GET YOUR MONEY RIGHT

EMMANUEL ASUQUO is a qualified financial advisor and has worked in financial services for over fifteen years. He works with individuals and businesses to help them manage their money. He has worked for HSBC, NatWest, HBOS and Barclays, before becoming an independent financial advisor. He has been featured in *The Times*, *Telegraph*, *The Sun* and *Daily Mail* newspapers and has been invited to speak as an expert guest on BBC Radio on multiple occasions. Emmanuel featured as one of four experts on the popular Channel 4 finance show *Save Well, Spend Less* and on *Secret Spenders*. He was also an expert for the BBC One show *Your Money and Your Life* and featured on ITV's *This Morning*. He is a regular on the *Jeremy Vine* show on Channel 5.

GET YOUR MONEY RIGHT

Understand Your Money And Make It Work For You

EMMANUEL ASUQUO

WILLIAM COLLINS

William Collins
An imprint of HarperCollins*Publishers*
1 London Bridge Street
London SE1 9GF

WilliamCollinsBooks.com

HarperCollins*Publishers*
Macken House, 39/40 Mayor Street Upper
Dublin 1, D01 C9W8, Ireland

First published in Great Britain in 2023 by William Collins
This William Collins paperback edition published in 2024

1

A catalogue record for this book is available from the British Library

ISBN 978-0-00-858440-5

The information in this book is for general guidance and educational purposes only.
It is not a source of financial or legal advice. Any adjustments to your financial strategy or
plan should be undertaken only after consulting with a professional. In addition, neither
HarperCollins nor the Author offer investment advice and all financial investments
carry risk. You should therefore also seek independent financial advice before making
any investment. HarperCollins and the Author make no guarantee of positive
financial results by using the methods illustrated in this book.

Set in Adobe Garamond

Printed and bound in the UK using 100% renewable electricity at CPI Group (UK) Ltd

This book contains FSC™ certified paper and other controlled
sources to ensure responsible forest management

For more information visit: www.harpercollins.co.uk/green

I dedicate this book to my children,
Malachi, Ethan, Eliora and Mia-Rae.
You have always been my 'why', you motivate me to
push boundaries and do things I never thought possible.
One of my biggest achievements is being your father;
never stop dreaming!

Contents

Introduction

I'm writing this book to empower people and help them to change their mindsets. I grew up on a council estate in Tower Hamlets, which is a place where nobody really talks about anything other than money – and those who want to make it (legally) talk about 'making it' to Canary Wharf, where they believe everyone gets rich. I thought that way too. I just needed to get there, and I'd be rich. I remember looking out of my bedroom window, beyond the grey silhouette of the tower blocks that surrounded me, and seeing the Barclays tower shining bright against the night sky, and thinking how badly I wanted to get over there. I wanted to start making big money. With a lot of hard work, I did make it over there.

I entered my new career feeling like I knew the deal and that I was all lined up to start stacking some proper numbers, but I quickly realised I'd entered a whole different world. There were a whole load of things I'd never even heard of before, things that nobody I knew was doing. No wonder everyone but the drug dealers on the block were broke. All these people in Canary Wharf knew all this stuff, but nobody was sharing this information with people I knew. It never left this already privileged community. I want to change that.

I do what I do because I want to share this previously inaccessible information, and in the right way – a relatable way that the people I know can understand. I've read countless money books, and they're great, but a lot of them are written in a way that I can't really relate to – I can't see myself in these situations, nor can I see anyone I grew up with in them. I want to tell stories where people can see themselves and therefore really understand and relate to the knowledge they need to improve their lives. They don't need to relate to them directly, either: they may read one of my stories and think, 'Ah yeah I've got an uncle/sister/brother/dad/cousin like that.' For me, financial education is something that should be taught in the home, not just in schools. It's an essential life skill that a huge percentage of the population aren't even close to having. You've got guys out there just splashing their pay cheque via various Buy Now Pay Later schemes to fund shoes that everyone assumes are fake anyway. People are thinking, those Gucci shoes aren't real, he works for Tesco. Little do they know, my man has splashed two-thirds of his wages just to look like a BTEC rapper.

It means a lot to be here and have the chance to write this book. I see it as my chance to help normal people feel like they have some say when it comes to money – even as a fully qualified financial adviser, it's taken me fifteen years to finally feel like the industry respects me. The other day, they were talking about gas prices going up on the news and I had Sky, ITV and Channel 4 all asking for my opinion – it's mad, like finally I've been accepted; before, it felt like there was no chance of this sort of thing happening for me. It was all rich old white guys on my screen, and to be honest, while I was interested in the subject they were discussing, I often switched off – I couldn't relate. Financial knowledge felt like it was for the elite. Suddenly, things changed – suddenly, everyone wants to hear about what's happening with my clients, the people I work with, as they are the sort of people that are going to be most impacted by things like the rising cost of petrol – what's 20p extra a litre to a multi-millionaire, after all. My clients need the financial advice they're given to be engaging and relevant to their day to day. Otherwise they'll switch off and won't learn what they need to do to better their circumstances – I want to give these people hope. This book is for anyone who wants, or, more realistically, needs, to get their money right. I know I joke around online, but I really care about this stuff. I live for it.

When it comes to financial education, I hear a lot of complaining. A lot of blaming other people, and a lot of victimhood. We're just waiting on schools and the government to step in and save the day here, but for me it's down to us. We need to learn and build the knowledge for ourselves. But where do you start? I want this book to be that place. I use normal, everyday language and normal examples of everyday people. People that you can look at and be like, 'Yeah, I know that situation', and fully understand where the person in the case study has gone wrong, and then use it to inform your own decisions. Wealth is attainable for all of us. So is the lifestyle we all want. I can help you live the life you're pretending to live on Instagram; you just need to listen. My people, I can help you change your life! Where you are today does not need to define where you are tomorrow. Take the time to read this book and make the changes.

A lot of other money books just give you knowledge – knowledge which is hard to relate to and hard to understand. I am going to give you that knowledge in a way you *can* understand, and I am also going to give you the practical steps you can take to actually create change for yourself. I'm not just being kind, I'm getting paid for this. So, you gon' learn today, but you're also going to enjoy doing it. And you're going to love the results. You know what, this book isn't just about money; it's about legacy – think of your children, and your grandchildren, and how much they'll rate you for setting them up financially. Rather than being dead grandparent *yourname* who left behind a mountain of debt and some crusty slippers. I don't want you to be a financial burden.

Look, I'm realistic. I know the pressure we're all under. Much as we might not like to admit it, many of us subscribe to conventional definitions of success in some way or another. It takes a huge amount of self-control, planning and financial education to not keep up with the Joneses, the Chans, the Amfos, the Singhs, or the Babawales. Systemic narratives and cultural pressures lead us to misguidedly believe that buying the latest handbag, owning the newest car or taking luxury holidays is a sure-fire route to happiness. While these things may contribute to a happy lifestyle, if that's what you care about, they are not the be-all and end-all. If all we do is spend our money, we are simply lining the pockets of wealthy companies and leaving ourselves with nothing left to invest.

I am going to help you unlearn these bad habits and talk about the misconceptions which have kept you from achieving the financial security you so desire – the financial security you need. I'm always telling people the person who is stealing your money is *you*, because, if most of us reflect on why we are living pay cheque to pay cheque, have very little saved or are in debt, it's not the fault of advertising, social media or even society. Ultimately the responsibility lies with us.

We are the ones making the spending decisions, we are the ones choosing whether or not to save and invest, and we are the ones in control of our financial futures. This book is designed to take you from wherever you are financially to a place where you are in CONTROL of your money, so that you can earn more of it, build wealth and finally, as I said before (remember the slippers), pass it on to the next generation. I've made this book as accessible as possible – so whether you're spending all your money on Uber Eats and needlessly expensive gym memberships (is that steam room really helping to tone your arms and shift belly fat) or using the bank's overdraft (the overdraft is not your money) to book trips to Dubai, this book is for you. I am going to give you the knowledge you need to take control of your finances. I take complicated financial principles and break them down into practical, easy-to-understand concepts; I may be an Instagram superstar, but believe me, I'm a certified financial adviser too, and I do this well – I had to pass my financial advice qualifications. I will also be sharing stories of clients I have helped and the mess they were in before they met me, giving specific insight into how I helped them out of their situation. Usually, with money, you need to learn from your mistakes, but now you can just read this book and learn from other people's and the advice of a qualified financial adviser. I can confirm that this is a good investment – well done.

I want you to understand that there is no obligation to read this from cover to cover or all in one go. It has been written so you can dip in and out and come back to sections as you embark upon your financial journey. If you want to buy a house, we have a chapter on that, and if you're investing for the first time, there is also a chapter for you.

1

The UK
Financial System

What is the barter economy?

All right, before we talk about how to get your money right, let's talk about what money actually *is*. People have traded since the beginning of time, but back in the day people didn't use money. They used a system called barter. Never heard of the barter system? Let Eman explain it to you.

Today, let's say you want to buy some groceries. You roll up to the shop, drop your coins or tap your card and transfer money from your bank account into the supermarket's bank account. The supermarket can then use that money to buy more produce to sell on, pay its staff – and those staff can use that money to pay their rent, their bills and so forth. But it hasn't always been like that.

Before the invention of money, people used to trade products and services with each other directly. This made a lot more sense in simpler times, when communities were smaller and there was no Instagram or Snapchat. This means that if you were someone who produced rice and you needed some clothes, you would use that rice to trade directly with someone who knew how to sew.

The barter economy became too limited

The barter system makes sense when you're dealing with groups of tens or hundreds of people, but this becomes way harder in more complex societies made up of thousands or millions of people. This is the reality in many of the countries around the world today. Many of us don't even know the people who live on our street, let alone the people we live in the same country as. Let's use the same example from earlier – what if you are a person who produces rice, but you need clothes and shoes? Now you're running around town barefoot, trying to find a person (or people) who can make both of those things, hoping that they don't already have rice at home.

So some very clever people came up with the idea that we should trade our goods and service for what's called a 'medium of exchange'. This is where you trade goods and services for something valuable – could be precious metals, stones or shells – and then those precious items can be traded for something else further down the line. So now our rice producer can use this medium of exchange to buy their shoes and clothes flexibly, and the person they buy them from can trade with someone else in the future.

What is money?

Way, way, way before bitcoin (calm down people, we're going to get on to cryptocurrency in a minute) the first known currency, the shekel, was created in Mesopotamia – the area that we now call modern Iraq – 5,000 years ago. I often speak to people who don't like money or think it's the root of all evil. But whatever you think about it, money is a very old concept, and it's a part of our lives, like it or not. So for as long as it's here, you're going to have to learn how to handle it, or else it will handle you.

Money does three very important jobs in a financial system, and I'm going to explain them to you using the trusty plantain. If you don't know what plantain is – put this book down immediately and google it. I'll be here waiting for you when you get back.

Medium of exchange: so let's say you wanted to get your hands on some delicious plantain. Rather than having to barter for it as described before, you can use money to buy four plantains for £1. The person you've bought it from can use that money to transact with other people as well.

Unit of account: money lets us know how much stuff costs compared to other stuff. The amount of money you'd be willing to spend on four plantains is probably a lot less than the amount you'd spend on a car or a holiday, no matter how delicious plantain is. We use money to give value to things based on demand and supply.

Store of value: money helps us to value things over time. A currency would be absolutely useless if you used it to buy some plantain today but went to the shop next week and the supermarket rejected your hard-earned coins because they weren't worth anything any more. Trust me, in some countries this actually happens. In January 2022 one pound sterling was around 560 naira (the currency of Nigeria). So money acts as a 'store of value', because we can use it to value things now and in the future.

Jeez! All this talk of plantain is making my belly rumble!

Gold standard

So now you're feeling all clever because you're clued-up on how money works. Over time many things have been used as money, but a very popular medium of exchange has been gold. Why gold? Because it is a rare, precious metal that is difficult to mine but can also be used in the real world. Gold is used in everything from jewellery to dentistry to microchips. But one of its main uses in the past was as a way for people to trade with one another, and it was often minted into coins.

But gold has one massive weakness. My goodness, gold is heavy! Back in the day, people literally had to be able to 'flex' if they wanted to flex because carrying gold around was not easy. So over time, banks and financial institutions started to store gold safely in vaults and instead create paper money in place of the gold, which was easier to carry around. Banks were not allowed to create more paper money than the amount of physical gold they actually had. This was to stop the money in the system losing its value, which was called the 'gold standard'.

It was a very simple way for countries to measure the value of their currencies against one another.

Fiat money

This all came to an end in 1931, thirteen years after the end of the First World War, when the UK and many countries around the world came off the gold standard. Long story short – wars are very expensive, and to stop themselves from running out of money, many countries started to print more money than the amount they had available in physical gold. Today, money is nothing more than a series of digits on a screen, created by central banks around the world. In the UK our central bank is the Bank of England and it is tightly controlled by interest rates.

If the money supply is too high, the Bank of England will stop creating money and will increase interest rates, to encourage people to reduce spending and to save their cash instead. And if the money supply is too low, the Bank of England will increase the amount of money in the system and reduce interest rates to get people spending again. If this sounds like madness to you, this is how the modern financial system works. The money we all work hard to earn and spend on our everyday necessities isn't tied to anything any more. This is called 'fiat' money. And no, I'm not talking about your uncle's Punto.

Cryptocurrency

If the Mesopotamian shekel was the first ever currency, then cryptocurrency is the most recent. There are 180 currencies in the world, from euros to dollars to naira, but there are thousands of cryptocurrencies. My goodness, it seems like a new cryptocurrency is coming out every week! So we're just going to talk about the biggest one – bitcoin. Bitcoin was created in 2009 and was the first cryptocurrency ever. It was created by a person, or group, called Satoshi Nakamoto – nobody knows who they are yet – as a way for people to be able to send money to each other person-to-person, over a network called the blockchain.

Once transactions are recorded on the blockchain, they can't be edited, making this a simple way to transfer and make payments without the need for a bank. New bitcoin are created through a process called 'mining', which is where computers on the blockchain network verify the transactions that are made and earn new coins as a reward. Bitcoin was also designed to be finite, and so all the bitcoin ever created will be successfully mined by around 2140. Part of the reason why bitcoin is so popular is because, unlike fiat money, you can't just create more and more of it. It's difficult to mine and can be used in the real world, like gold.

How does the banking system work?

You might be wondering at this point, how do central banks 'create money'? Out of thin air? The short answer is yes. The slightly longer answer is that they create money by lending it out at interest. Central banks can introduce more money into the system by lending it, either to governments or to commercial banks. Although the borrowers need to pay this money back in the future at an agreed date it can be many years away, meaning that they can spend and benefit from the money in the meantime.

But governments can't just take this money willy-nilly. They have to create what's called a 'bond' – and I'm not talking about Idris Elba (can he just hurry up and accept the role already?!). The easiest way to think of a bond is as an IOU note. So let's imagine I wanted to lend £100 to the government: they would have to create an IOU note saying, 'I promise to pay Emmanuel £100 back in twelve months' time.' The government would get the money and I would get the IOU – which would be worth £100, because this is the amount they have agreed to pay back to me.

Printing money

Governments do this to raise money all the time. Commercial banks and companies do this too, and when we get on to the credit section in this book, I will teach you how you can use debt to your advantage in this way as well. For now, just know that bonds that are used by governments are all 'government bonds' and bonds that are used by companies are called 'corporate bonds'. When people use the phrase 'printing money', this is what they are talking about – the lending of money by central banks to commercial banks and governments. A consequence of new money being introduced into the system in this way is inflation. I don't use the word 'consequence' in a good or a bad way, because our financial system has got us to where we are today.

While not perfect, in the UK we do have a good standard of living, and free healthcare and education for all. But adding new money into the system is one of the causes of inflation: pumping new money into the system causes the money that's already in the system to lose its value. Imagine the most expensive exclusive pair of designer trainers you can think of – there are only a handful of pairs of its kind in the world. Well, if you were to mass-produce these same trainers, you could probably expect the value of all the trainers to fall, as there are now so many more on the market. This is exactly what happens with money, but much more slowly. In fact, the Bank of England has an annual inflation target of 2 per cent. In simple terms it means that each year your money will be able to buy about 2 per cent less than it could a year before.

What is tax?

Governments raise money from central banks, but that's not the only way they do it. Anyone who has had the joy of looking at their payslip on payday will know all too well that there is no such thing as earning 100 per cent of your money. The government will always take their cut, and this is what we call tax. Like the invention of money itself, tax is a very old concept. The first tax systems were created in Ancient Egypt around 3,000 years ago. There are many different types of taxes today, but the concept remains the same. Tax is a way for governments to raise money from their citizens, to be used on public services and infrastructure – roads, bin collection, railways, and so on. The government department responsible for collecting tax in the UK is called His Majesty's Revenue and Customs, or HMRC for short.

Governments raise and lower taxes to encourage different types of behaviour and spending. A good example is cigarettes. Because governments want to discourage people from smoking, the amount of tax you pay on a £14 packet of cigarettes is a huge 16.5 per cent (£2.31) of the overall price on a packet of twenty. They will then use these tax revenues on the associated healthcare costs and on programmes to help people quit. By comparison, there is a zero rate of tax on fruit and vegetables. You'd better all be getting your five a day – Eman is watching you! For the different types of tax we pay, see the section at the end of this chapter.

Producers and consumers

One thing you must understand about our financial system is that it's made of two groups of people – producers and consumers. Simply put, there are the people that make stuff and the people that buy stuff. They aren't mutually exclusive – you can be both a producer and a consumer, but the thing is, if you want to succeed in this system you've got to be a net consumer. Believe me when I say it's a jungle out here.

Think of all the time you spend on social media. Social media seems like it's free, but it's not. It's been said that if you're using a free product, 'you're not the customer; you're the product being sold'. You can spend hours and hours consuming social media and have nothing much to show for it. Meanwhile, my man Mark Zuckerberg is a multi-billionaire. There is no difference between you and Mark, other than that he made something for people to use, and you are the person using it.

Here's another example. Think about when, in 2020, we were worried that the economy was going to fail because of back-to-back coronavirus lockdowns. What did the government create? Eat Out to Help Out. The government loves to get us spending, and I actually respected them because they didn't even try and hide it.

Now there's nothing wrong with spending money. In a system of producers and consumers, you need people to spend money or the whole thing will grind to a halt. But if all you do with your money is spend it – if you don't use it to save or invest, or to build businesses – you will not get very far. There will always be people eager for you to spend your money with them. So you've got to be vigilant. As with everything in life, it's all about balance.

How to get your money right

I've written this book to give you a complete picture of all the different ways you can use money. So yes, we're going to talk about how to spend it on things that enhance or add value to your life. But we're also going to talk about how to borrow it responsibly, how to use money to make more money either through business, saving or investing, and how to create and pass on generational wealth.

When I talk about generational wealth you might think that I am talking about money itself. This is definitely a part of it. But there is no generational wealth without education. So we're going to talk about what it means to be financially literate in the next chapter.

Let me tell you a story about the six-figure earner

Let me tell you about Jerome. Jerome is a nice guy, always been a hard worker, focused on building money, focused on growing, but he's never been the main earner.

Jerome has always seen everybody around him make him money. And he's always thought, 'One day, I'm gonna make money', so he set himself a goal of making £120k a year. And he thought, 'You know, once I make £120k a year, I'm going to live in the type of house I want, I can drive the type of car I want, I can finally talk to the type of girls that I want.' You see, in his mind he's limited in the type of woman he can talk to because of the amount of money that he's making. If only he could just make £120k, he could talk to any girl, and they'd be on it.

So he starts working hard. He gets into work early, does all his tasks, helps his boss, does his boss's tasks, works extra hours after work.

Finally he gets some great news – he gets a promotion and has been given a £120k salary! For the first time ever, the world is a different place. Jerome is walking differently now – that £120k walk! The air he breathes is different. Although he hasn't told anyone he's on £120k he feels that he can command more respect from people (even though, in reality, no one knows what his salary actually is).

But another thing happens. All of a sudden he believes he now has 'haters'. From Jerome's perspective, suddenly everybody's watching him. Everybody's clocking him. Now he feels like he has to do stuff to prove his 'haters' wrong.

So he buys clothes. But he feels like he can't wear them more than once, because he's been seen in them and he doesn't want people to think he's poor. He changes his car. He originally had a Ford Focus (which he loved), but now he's on £120k the Ford Focus is an embarrassment. So he gets himself a BMW.

Jerome is also living with his mum. But because of his new salary, he decides he can't live with his mum any more. So instead he rents a nice apartment in the city near his office. This way, he thinks, he can stay late after work, go to bars and the clubs with his colleagues and he doesn't have to worry about public transport any more.

So Jerome's now got a new car and a new apartment – did I forget to tell you about his new model girlfriend too? Whenever he takes his girlfriend out he pays for everything – expensive restaurants, expensive gifts. Remember that Jerome hasn't actually received his first pay cheque yet. But in his mind, when £120k hits his bank account he will be just fine. He has already calculated that his new pay cheque will be about £10,000 a month.

A few weeks later, payday comes and he goes to check his bank account. Confused, he sees a figure of just over £5,000 (£5,214 to be exact). It turns out the taxman has taken almost half of the money. National Insurance – gone. Pension contributions – gone. Plan 2 student loan – gone!

Jerome realises that once he factors in all the extra hours he is doing in his new role there's not that much difference between what he's taking home now and what he was taking home before. He was on 60k and was taking home £3,209 a month, but at least he could actually enjoy his evenings, and his expenses were nothing compared to what they are now.

So what's the moral of this story? Firstly, you can't define yourself by the amount of money that you're making. Sometimes it can feel like the more you're paid, the better you're doing in life – but the thing is, you were already doing great. Jerome was already doing great! But now Jerome's got a car costing him £500 a month, he's spending £2,000 a month on dates with his girlfriend, and pays rent of almost £3,000 a month. And because he didn't plan for deductions to his salary, now he's having to use credit cards and overdrafts to maintain his six-figure lifestyle.

So it's really important that you give yourself credit for where you are, while also trying to build. Jerome had the right work ethic and he had the right mentality. However, when he made more money, he should have kept his expenses the same. That way, when he earned more, he would have kept more. And because of his salary level, he could have focused on buying a property. You can get a great mortgage on a £120k salary.

If you're happy with your current lifestyle, there is no need to start adding all these costs. Like the old saying – money comes and money goes. One day you're on £120k, and the next (heaven forbid) you're made redundant and then you can't afford anything any more. I know this – I got made redundant from my job as a financial adviser in 2019.

The key to being happy is to know your worth and know your value. It's not based on what your salary is, what car you can drive or the house you live in. It's based on who you are, without all those things.

The types of tax we pay

There are many different types of tax we pay in the UK, so let's talk about the main ones. First of all there's **Income Tax** – as the name suggests, this is a tax you pay when you receive income. This can be from your salary, from dividends, or when you withdraw from your pension. Generally speaking, the higher your income, the greater the proportion of Income Tax you have to pay.

Next there's **National Insurance (NI)** – a tax that was created in 1911, to protect working people against loss of income either due to sickness or unemployment. If you've heard of Social Security in the US, the two are very similar. National Insurance is normally taxed on salaries, but you can also choose to make NI contributions voluntarily if you're not earning a salary, e.g. if you've taken time out of work for childcare purposes.

When you buy a house, flat, land or other building types in the UK you have to pay a **property tax** to the government. This is called Stamp Duty Land Tax (SDLT, or just Stamp Duty for short), and is dependent on the price of the property. If that property goes up in price and you sell it at a profit, you may have to pay a proportion of your profit to the government as **Capital Gains Tax**. Assets include stocks and shares, but also second homes and buy-to-let property. There are some exceptions to this, but you pay Capital Gains Tax as a percentage of the money you have made on the asset.

When you next go to a restaurant, look at the bill. You will see that a proportion of the price is made up of **Value-Added Tax**, VAT. VAT is added to the purchase price of certain kinds of goods and services, meaning that if you buy those items, you are paying a form of tax.

And now for possibly the most bizarre type of tax. When you die, you have to pay tax – can you imagine! **Inheritance Tax** (IHT as it's sometimes called for short) is charged as a percentage of the value of your assets (called your estate) over a certain amount. You may be thinking, 'Oh my lord, even in death I cannot escape tax?!', but look at it this way: if the government is coming for your money in death, it is because you've achieved something great in life. There are ways to legally avoid or reduce Inheritance Tax, and don't worry, Eman is going to teach you about some of these in this book.

Lastly, let's not forget that companies pay **Corporation Tax** on their profits. This is the money that is remaining after they have earned revenues and covered their costs. Generally, bigger businesses pay a higher rate of Corporation Tax than smaller businesses, and it's charged as a percentage of the profit earned. Whenever you hear people grumbling that companies are not paying their fair share of tax, it is Corporation Tax they are normally talking about.

2

Financial Education in the UK

Why aren't we taught about money at school?

If I'm gonna be real, I wasn't always the most gifted at school. I was far too interested in getting the latest pair of basketball trainers or chasing after girls, especially when I was in secondary school. So it was difficult to be engaged in any subject my teachers were trying to teach me. Maybe that's because school was far more interested in teaching me about Shakespeare and Pythagoras' theorem than essential life skills which I would definitely need to use in my life, like understanding how debt works, or how to read a payslip.

Now don't get me wrong: teaching is one of the most important professions on earth, and the teachers that taught me, and the teachers I now know as an adult, are some of the most hard-working people I know. Teachers toil all hours under the sun, and barely get the pay to reflect their labour. But the education system could do a lot more to prepare young people for adult life, particularly when it comes to understanding how money works. I went through the entire school system without receiving a single lesson on how to use a credit card. No wonder that when I first got my hands on one, I immediately went into debt. I haven't always been as financially literate as I am now. Back in my younger days, I was moving mad!

Debt is an industry

Now I'm not big on conspiracy theories, but my guess as to why we're not taught about money at school is because there are a lot of people (with money) who don't want regular people on the street understanding how the financial system works in case, heaven forbid, they make some money, too. Understand, my people, that the debt industry is exactly that – an industry. According to IBIS World, the revenues of the Debt Collection Agencies industry grew 17.5 per cent to £1.9 billion in 2022. I am all for businesses making money, and, as we will go on to talk about in this book, it is possible to use debt responsibility, but right now the debt industry makes a lot of money from your financial mistakes.

The thing is, we can't afford not to teach young people about money at school. Not everyone is lucky enough to come from a family that understands money, and so our education system helps to level the playing field for people who might not be able to learn about money in the home. School can also help to provide a way for children to learn about money in a way that's up to date. When I was young, I used to have to pay for the bus in cash (40p for a child's fare and 70p for an adult

– if you know, you know!) and I remember my mum swiping her card and signing receipts at Tesco whenever she paid for groceries using a bank card. Now everything is cashless, so the lessons we should be teaching need to be updated.

Opportunity cost of introducing financial literacy

There is a huge cost if we do not teach young people about money, and how to be self-sufficient. The example I would use is one around health. Back in 2005, Jamie Oliver launched the Feed Me Better campaign to get healthy food served in schools, to tackle child obesity, with great success. Parents can send their children to school safe in the knowledge that they are getting a fresh, cooked meal. Now, we could have decided to let those children become unhealthy, then grow into unhealthy adults, and then make money off those adults by charging them for weight-loss programmes and healthcare. But I think the world is a much better place for having more healthy people in it who can be active participants in our economy, rather than victims of it.

It's a shame that we are in a place where we would rather make money off people's lack of financial awareness rather than level the playing field and make money off people's financial intelligence. Imagine if every child left school with a full understanding of how saving and investing worked, how to buy property and how to start and build a business. Isn't that a world you'd want to live in? The thought of that excites me, personally. And it is why I get out of bed every morning.

How to help teachers when it comes to financial literacy

One of the first steps to increasing the amount of financial education in schools is to enhance teachers' own confidence when it comes to financial literacy. Right now, we are in a bit of a chicken and egg situation where the people we would need to teach this stuff in school haven't been taught themselves. According to the Money and Pensions Service, only three- fifths (59 per cent) of schools and colleges feel they have the necessary knowledge and skills to support their learners develop financial skills, and less than half (49 per cent) had a good understanding of which external agencies provide money advice or financial education and are able to signpost learners to them.

Now I know I might sound biased, but I think that while we are in this middle stage of trying to increase everyone's financial literacy (both the students' and the teachers') we should invite external organisations and individuals to come into schools and deliver financial literacy workshops, using content created by trusted voices in the UK as teaching resources. Shoutout organisations like MyBnk, for example, do this for young people in the UK. On social media, where I do a lot of my work, there are many, many great content creators who break down financial concepts in an easy-to-understand, fun way, using everything from TikTok videos to short explainer videos and infographics, suitable for children and adults alike.

Cost of financial literacy – where does the funding come from?

'But Eman!', I hear you say. 'How are schools supposed to pay for all these workshops? Won't this be expensive?' And I think you're absolutely right. Private schools and academies already receive funding, so for them it is just a case of making more time available in the syllabus for financial education to be taught. For state and non-fee-paying schools, however, someone will need to pay for all this external education, and I think it's only right that it is funded by financial companies. Yep – I said it! Banks, investment companies, fintechs, property companies, loan and credit providers. In my view, if these companies are going to benefit financially from today's children one day growing up and using their products and services, then it is only right that they devote a percentage of their revenues to help educate their future customers in a responsible way.

I have worked with many financial brands in my job as a financial adviser and content creator, but also when teaching workshops and putting on events. In my view, if financial brands helped to sponsor workshops in schools, or provided funding to charities and social enterprises who are doing the work already, it's a win-win for everyone. The schools and education providers get the funding for high-quality financial education, and the pupils and teachers get indirect advertising towards financial products and services they will likely go on to use as adults. This has already started to happen in the work I am doing, and I would like to see it continue.

Financial education should be taught in the home

Another important place for financial education to be taught is in the home. As a father of four children, I have seen first-hand how early on children become aware of money as a concept – particularly when it comes to them wanting to buy or be bought things! I understand that not every household is going to have the time or knowledge to teach their children about money, but it's important that we try to do this because the children are going to pick things up anyway, whether we take the time to teach them or not.

Teaching children about money doesn't have to be complicated, and it doesn't have to be a hush-hush subject. Something that has worked for me is using what I like to call 'financial touchpoints' to involve the children in money decisions whenever they come up in daily life. There are many more of these than you might at first think. It could be as simple as letting your children know how much things cost whenever you take them to the supermarket. Or explaining to them the cost of energy and bills in the home – especially if you have a smart meter, because it will display the price of the amount of gas and electricity you are using on a daily basis. Starting these conversations early will help your children to appreciate how much stuff costs and will empower them to make financial decisions as they grow up.

Teach kids how to make money and add value (e.g. making cakes)

It doesn't all have to be about spending when teaching kids about money; you can also teach them how to add value and make money too. My wife bakes cakes (and if you don't mind me saying, they are the most delicious cakes you will ever taste in your life. Check them out at @mimitoyoucakes on Instagram). So when she bakes, sometimes she will involve the children and give them cakes to sell at school. By doing this, she shows them how they can make money by buying the raw ingredients at the supermarket and then turning them into something that people are willing to pay for. It also helps the children to build relationships at school, because the cakes are so good!

There is a US creator on social media called Gary Vaynerchuk. He curses a lot, but aside from that I really like him. He does a lot of great content on how to make money doing car boot sales. Another idea you could try to teach your kids, made popular by Gary V, is to get items that are listed for free on Facebook Marketplace, eBay and Gumtree and then try to sell them at a profit. When people list stuff for free on online marketplaces, it's often because they are trying to declutter but don't necessarily want to throw away their belongings. So it's another win-win. You get an item for free, the seller gets a bit more space in their house, and you can then sell on that item at a profit; your children grow to understand the real-world importance of being able to add value. What better way for your child to get some or all of their pocket money than to earn it?

Teach kids how to give back

A final, very important thing to teach kids is how to give back. My parents were able to give me a better upbringing than they got when they were growing up, and I am very fortunate to be able to give my children the same. (There was no PlayStation in my house when I was coming up, trust me!) So something I am conscious of is that I don't want my children to grow up thinking that stuff just 'appears' when you ask for it, or that every child has the same opportunities.

So try to think of ways to get your family involved in activities that give back. This could be by volunteering at a local church or food bank, or encouraging them to donate part of their pocket money to a charitable cause.

Parents should get educated themselves

As a parent, if you don't feel very confident speaking about money, or maybe your parents didn't teach you about money themselves, then it's up to you to get educated. In financial education there is a concept called 'paying yourself first' (see page 98), which basically means that when you get paid you allocate a portion of your income to savings, no matter what. You're paying yourself before you give your money to anyone else – the credit card company, the supermarket, ASOS or whatever. Well, the same is true in terms of how you spend your time. Before you give all your time to *Love Island* or aimless social media scrolling, try to take some time out every day to invest in yourself. You're reading this book, that is a good start! But there are also many great money podcasts, YouTube channels and social media pages you can follow in order to continue your financial education journey. The key is to be intentional and understand how you work best.

If you're more of an audio learner, then podcasts and audiobooks are for you. If you prefer to go into the detail, then books and online articles might be better suited to you. Small things that you add to your knowledge base will build over time and increase your confidence when it comes to teaching your kids. Don't forget: while there are financial principles which will stand the test of time, the world of finance is moving far too quickly for everyone to know everything and have all the answers, and you know how your children learn best. The most important thing is that you feel empowered to teach them, and hopefully, between the lessons they are receiving at school and what you are teaching them at home, your children will grow into self-sufficient, financially empowered adults.

Let me tell you a story about teaching your children about money

One of the big things my wife and I find with our kids is that they can like something one day and hate it the next. For example, one day they love tomato ketchup, but the next day it's disgusting and they don't want to have anything to do with it. And we have four kids, so if everyone decides that something's bad, the money we paid for it goes down the drain. So we like to get the kids involved when it comes to doing the shopping list, but also to allocate them a budget for part of it. They can decide how many snacks they get each week, and we give them money towards them so they can then work out between themselves what they want. Giving them this auton-omy makes later discussions easier. When we sit down and say, 'Look, this is what you're eating this evening,' they can't turn round and say they don't want it, because they've been part of the selection process. For us as parents this is great for plan-ning, and means we avoid food waste.

Also we have a 'star' reward system, so if they finish their meals, wash their plates or tidy up, they get stars, and those stars relate to their pocket money. Our children also know that when it comes to money they shouldn't spend all of it at once. We encourage them to split it into three: 50 per cent goes into a jar for stuff they want to buy straight away, 40 per cent for bigger items they're saving for, and 10 per cent is always about giving back.

We don't mind if it's giving to charity, or giving back to the church – it can be whatever cause they want, but it's import-ant that they know there's no such thing as spending 100 per cent of your income. Number one, you spend some of it on your present self; number two, you pay your future self; and number three, you give back.

When it comes to involving them in household costs, our smart meter tells us how much energy is being used, where; so we can work out, for example, if they leave the light on in their room and then come downstairs for an hour, how much that costs. Therefore we're able to make them conscious of wasting water, wasting electricity, wasting gas, and the financial impact that has.

Finally – and this is a big one – we always encourage our children to make money. If they see ways in which they can make money, we will always support them. For example, they were doing a sale at their school, and one of my sons bought sweets and crisps and then sold them. As has just been explained, some of that money was donated to the school, but he got to keep the rest of the profits, and then I matched what he made so that he earned double.

At other times, to make money, the kids sell unwanted items such as toys, clothes or video games on resell sites or sell them to their friends, and again I've doubled their profits or paid back the amount it cost them to purchase the items. These are the types of things that we try to get them to understand – that you can use money to make you money. This shows the importance of splitting up your income, and not spending all your money on instant gratification – and also the importance of adding value to people.

3

Money Mindset

Let's talk about money mindset

In this chapter we're going to talk about mindset. Before we can even get into the numbers, it's very important that we talk about your mind. Because if your mind's not in the right place and you're not doing things for the right reasons, when it comes down to it you're not going to be able to make your best financial decisions. And when I talk about this, I always use the example of cigarette packets. Anyone who's seen a cigarette packet will know that it has a big warning message that says 'SMOKING KILLS', but despite this people continue to smoke while still wanting to quit. This isn't because they're bad people, it's because knowing that what you *should* do is a very different issue to knowing *why* you're doing it. So before we talk about anything else, we're going to talk about knowing your 'why'. This is a principle I have lived by for many years.

The importance of knowing your 'why'

I don't have any tattoos, but if I was to get one, the phrase 'Know your "why"' would probably come in the top three phrases I would be willing to tattoo permanently on my body. What a lot of us need to realise is that we are constantly relying on external factors to tell us how we should be living our lives. This is important when we are children – our parents raise us, teach us right from wrong and how to look after ourselves, and our friends tell us what is cool and what isn't, and we soak up information from school, TV, books and so on. But there comes a point in your life – when you've grown up – where you have to go, 'OK, why do I believe what I believe? Why do I get up and go to work every day? What actually motivates me?' instead of relying on your family, friends and society to tell you the answers to these questions.

What's my 'why'?

'So what's your "why", Eman?' I hear you ask. Let me tell you! I grew up in a British-Nigerian household in East London. I had everything a child could want – two very loving parents, my younger sisters and many happy memories. But I also spent part of my childhood on a council estate in not the greatest part of London. I was teased at school for never having the best clothes or the newest toys, and we never really went on holiday. I am sure my parents did their best to protect me and my sister from the realities of our situation, but even from an early age I was aware that we often had to struggle to make ends meet. We simply did not have that much money. So while

I am extremely grateful to my parents for getting me and my sisters to where we are as adults, I wanted to build upon what they'd done, change my situation and give back. I wanted to give back to my parents. But now I am a father, I want to give back to my wife and children as well.

Why I signed a contract with myself

So what did I do? I made a promise to myself that I was going to change my situation and the lives of the people around me – the people I loved and held most dear. I signed a contract with myself saying, 'I, Emmanuel Asuquo, promise to achieve X, Y, Z by such and such a date, signed by Emmanuel Asuquo, in the presence of Emmanuel Asuquo.' It might sound like an abstract concept, but if you want to achieve something you're going to need accountability, either to your past self or to the people around you. And despite what you might think, contracts actually work – I'll prove it to you. There is a well-known phenomenon called 'Monday blues', which is that feeling you get on a Monday morning as you trudge to work in a job you dislike. When you hate your job it can feel a lot like the situation has been forced upon you, but the reality is that you signed a contract with them, you agreed to the hours and the job description, and the reason why you still go in is because of the powerful accountability which the contract provides. Comedian Jim Carrey famously wrote a cheque to himself in 1985, for $10 million 'acting services rendered'. He dated it 1995, ten years into the future, and kept it in his wallet at all times. Ten years later, in November 1994, Jim was cast in the movie *Dumb and Dumber* for $10 million. Why not sign a contract with yourself today? You just might get what you signed for.

Your 'why' is going to be useful when life gets hard

Knowing your 'why' is going to be useful when life gets hard – and trust me, if you've not had hard times yet, they will come. That's just life. Sometimes you feel motivated to do something, and that can feel amazing. Leaping out of bed to go to a new job, diligently studying on a course or for a uni degree, or putting the hours into a new business venture, and having all of that come easy is definitely the ideal situation. But sometimes life is going to hand you lemons and you're going to have to make lemonade whether you want to or not. Sometimes you will be too tired to get up for that early-morning meeting, you might be reading the driest textbook of all time, or you may struggle to find customers for your business. If you know your 'why', you will be able to push through the tough times and keep on going. Keep your 'why' as your north star – you're going to need it.

Create an evaluation framework

But how do you find out what your 'why' is? Another great question! Many of us lead busy lives, so it can be difficult to find the time to reflect and think about what we are really trying to get out of life. We get out of bed in the morning and go to work, not because we're trying to achieve some grand life goal but because we've got rent and bills to pay. I've been there before; I definitely get it. However, you need to find some time to reflect on your life so you can figure out what direction you would like to take it in. Figuring out your 'why' isn't easy, and it is likely to change over time as well. So you need to create what I like to call an 'evaluation framework'. An evaluation framework contains questions that you can ask yourself in order to get closer to your purpose.

Ask yourself some questions

Great questions to ask yourself are:

- What gets me out of bed in the morning?

- What things do I really want to change in my life?

- What causes me the most pain and discomfort on a day-to-day basis?

- What are the benefits of changing my situation?

- What does a new situation mean to me, how would it make me feel, how would it affect me and my loved ones?

Of these questions, pick three that resonate most with you (or you can tweak them so that they better suit your situation), grab a pen and paper and write the answers to your questions as you understand them. No judgement from yourself or worrying about what other people might think. Just answer them in a notebook; there are no right or wrong answers. Be true to yourself. You might be surprised by some of the conclusions you come to, and you might not want to admit some of them. It might turn out that one of the main things causing you pain in your life is your marriage. Or that changing your situation requires you to leave your job or change your diet. Remember, we aren't focusing on the externals any more. This is all about you and what you want to get from your life.

Where I grew up

So, going back to when I created my own evaluation framework and signed my contract with myself – and I'll be straight up – I had to admit to myself that I didn't like where I lived. In the council estate where I grew up during the 1990s there was no buzzer at the door, so anyone could just walk in from the street. There was a lot of crime, spit on the floor and one of those giant industrial waste bins which was used by the entire building. If you know, you know. Whenever we'd come home there'd be huge flies buzzing around and we'd have to bat them away with our hands; there were rats and mice in our house and in our building. And as you walked around the building there was the smell of other people's cooking – although I don't know what food it was supposed to be because it always smelt horrible. You get the picture. This was my pain, and once I acknowledged this pain for what it really was I could make a promise to myself that I was going to change my situation.

Make your goals bigger than yourself

Another way to figure out your 'why' is to make your goals bigger than yourself. A person will only dream as big as the number of people on whom they are trying to have a positive impact. As a child, your circle of impact is only as big as yourself. You don't really have the ability to see things from other people's perspectives, nor can you think that far into the future, and so your actions reflect this. You're mainly concerned with watching TV, playing with your friends, eating and doing what your teachers and parents tell you to. As you get older, though, you are better able to see things from other people's perspectives, your responsibilities increase and your priorities change. If I were to base my goals merely on me, then I would probably just go to work, earn enough to look after myself alone and think as far ahead as the next few weeks and months. But now that I have a wife and children to feed, my goals have risen to meet the challenge and I think much bigger. Whatever it is in your life that would help you to dream bigger, I encourage you to do so.

Show your loved ones what is possible

Once you learn how to dream bigger, an amazing thing happens. You actually start to inspire the people around you to do the same. People always say to me, 'Emmanuel, I want to follow my heart and do my dream job, but my parents want me to do something different.' Trust me, I have definitely been there. My parents sacrificed a whole lot to move here in the 1980s from Nigeria and, as I have previously said, even though there was an abundance of love in my household when I was growing up, there was not that much money. If you have had a similar experience to this, particularly if you grew up in an immigrant household, you've got to recognise that our parents were concerned with survival. They grew up in a very different time to ours and had the highly important job of putting food on the table and keeping the lights on. Because our parents made those sacrifices, we are now able to take the torch from them and build upon what they've done. We are now no longer concerned with surviving: our job is to make sure we're thriving. Show your parents, or anyone else who might object to your goals, what is possible.

My redundancy story

When I first got a job in finance after university, my mum was over the moon. She did the classic 'mum' thing of telling all her friends that her son worked in a bank, and she was understandably very proud of me. I worked in finance for twelve years until, guess what? They made me redundant in 2019, and they told me it was a 'business decision'. Thankfully I had got my finances sorted by then, so I was able to get through that difficult time, but I made the decision there and then that I wasn't going to put my financial destiny in the hands of an employer and that I wasn't going back. And my mum, whom I used to talk to every day, would ask me repeatedly, 'When are you getting another job? When are you getting another job?' She would ask me this out of love of course, but, as I said before, I had reached a point in my life where I had to show my mum what was possible. Fast-forward a few years later to today, with everything I have achieved as a business owner, and now my mum says, 'Thank God you have your own business.'

'Everything seems impossible until it's done'

Setting big goals can be daunting, and it can sometimes feel silly setting yourself a target that you yourself don't think you can achieve. However, we must remember the words of Nelson Mandela: 'It always seems impossible until it's done.' Think about all the seemingly 'impossible' things we have achieved as human beings over the centuries. For early humans it would have seemed crazy to think that we could ever fly planes, land on the moon or create the internet. All these things would just have been goals or ideas to someone, at some point. But we put our minds to them and we made them a reality. I personally think that anything is possible, and that if you can imagine something, you can probably bring it into existence. I used to be a sprinter when I was at school, and one of my favourite events was the 100 metres. Sometimes I think back to when Usain Bolt ran the 100 metres at the 2009 IAAF World Championships, setting a world record of 9.58 seconds; I never thought the record could be broken in my lifetime. In fact, the sprinters in that race collectively ran so fast that all except one of them did it in ten seconds or less, which is just crazy to think about. So, definitely, I live my life with the belief that anything is possible, and I recommend that you do to.

People told me I'd already 'won', but it wasn't enough

To dream bigger we also need to raise our standards. Back when I was working in finance and I had the banker's salary, the fancy car and the title, people used to tell me that I'd already 'won'. Maybe, from their perspective, I had, but it all depends on what you're aiming for. Back in the day I used to work for Barclays, but today I partner with Barclays. I've done a TV series with Barclays in collaboration with Channel 4. Channel 4?! Do you think that as a child I ever thought I would be on television? When my TV series launched, it was displayed on Barclays' intranet as a new initiative they were working on with me and two other financial experts. People I used to work with were contacting me telling me that my face was on their computer screen. And to be very honest with you, I have my sights set further still. So the key to dreaming big and hitting your goals is to be happy with where you are and celebrate your milestones, but also to never settle.

How bad do you want it? Do you really want it?

The final thing I'll say when it comes to achieving your goals is that you have to ask yourself, 'How badly do I want to achieve this thing?' Do you really want it? Talking is easy. Just think about the number of people who say they want to become a millionaire, but how many of them actually become one? You want to become a millionaire but are you dreaming millionaire dreams? Are you setting millionaire goals? Are you putting in millionaire hours? A lot of people say they want to become wealthy, but they don't want to put in the work. Not wanting something is absolutely fine, by the way. Not everyone has to have the same goals. But don't kid yourself by setting yourself other people's goals. Follow the steps we have spoken about in this chapter — set yourself an evaluation framework, dream big and set big goals; let that be the reason why you get out of bed every morning, and your life will begin to head in that direction.

Now that we've talked about the importance of changing your mindset, in the next chapter we will talk about putting your new way of thinking into practice. Once you've tapped into the right sort of mindset, you've got to follow it up with action!

Let me tell you a story about 'knowing your "why"'

For me, knowing your 'why' is vital. I feel like, when I first started, I was just doing what I thought everybody else was supposed to do. I didn't have a purpose. And I have this saying: 'When you can't be motivated, you have to be disciplined.' I have always had the kind of spirit whereby if people gave me external motivation, it would work for me. But when you get into the workplace, sometimes you don't have that positive energy, and it's at times like this that you must be disciplined. And what is going to keep you disciplined is 'knowing your "why"', knowing why you're doing what you're doing. My first 'why' was my mum. When I was younger my mum always spoke positively about me. My dad was more like your typical African dad: 'Read your book! Read your book!' and so on. But with my mum it was more, 'Don't worry, son, you're going to be great. You're my pension.' Ha! At that time I didn't even know what a pension was, but I knew I was my mum's pension.

I watched my mum work as a dinner lady. And, you know, she literally sacrificed her body to try and earn money. I mean, to the point where her knees gave out and she even needed an operation. And I remember telling myself, 'I've gotta make money so that this woman can stop working.' I remember, there were basketball camps I wanted to go to, and my parents couldn't afford them. And then my mum would work some sort of magic and suddenly I'd be able to go. That's the type of woman she is. So when it came to work, when I couldn't be motivated I was disciplined, focused, I set my alarms, I was positive at work, I was working harder than everyone else. And I could do this because I could see the bigger picture. As I got married and had kids, they are now my 'why'. When I see my kids in the morning, it makes me work harder. It makes me want to go and take on the day. When I look at my wife working hard, it makes me want to work harder so that I can provide for her and my kids.

Now I've been able to retire my mum and support her financially. My kids don't know struggle or poverty, and that fills me with pride. But it took years of hard work, rejection, failure, disciple, consistency and trusting the process. So I definitely encourage you to know your 'why' and stick to it. It's going to help you in the journey ahead. Always remember: when you can't be motivated, be disciplined.

4

Building Good Financial Habits

Comparison is the thief of joy

In his book, *The Story of Philosophy*, Will Durant famously said: 'We are what we repeatedly do. Excellence, then, is not an act, but a habit.' So what can we learn from this? Basically, your ability to get a handle on your finances is not going to be about a single decision that you make today, tomorrow or next week. It's actually going to be the result of repeated decisions you make over a period of months and years. It's like exercising. If you miss going to the gym one morning, that is very unlikely to leave you unfit, but you will definitely notice the effects of several years of not working out. If you want to improve your finances, then you're going to have to build good financial habits. And by the way, we all have financial habits; it's just that most of us don't have financial habits that serve us.

Don't believe everything you see on social media

One of the biggest issues when it comes to building good financial habits is comparison. As social beings, we are constantly looking to other people for what we should be, do and have. Before the days of the internet, you would compare yourself to the people you could physically see in the space around you. You would compare yourself to a small circle of family and friends, or to your village. Now, with the invention of the internet and social media, we are comparing ourselves to people all over the world, and I don't believe we are wired to cope with that. You can at any point go on your phone and see where someone from your school went on holiday, someone you've not seen for decades, and let that affect how you feel in the present moment. And this is happening to everyone – young, old, famous and unknown. So you've got to be very careful when it comes to comparison. The Joneses are no longer next door, they're in your newsfeed as well.

You can't compare yourself to everyone else

The thing is, you can't compare yourself to everyone else. When I was a kid the standard saying from parents used to be 'Don't believe everything you see on TV.' Now I say to my kids, 'Don't believe everything you see on social media.' What you often view on social media is a highlight reel of the best parts of someone else's life. A picture-perfect pose on the beach may have taken half an hour and hundreds of photos to get just right. Someone's story post of them popping bottles on a night out may have been shot in an empty club. Whatever it is you're seeing on social media, take it with a huge pinch of Maggi cubes, because not many people are posting about the argument they had with their fiancé last week before they posted their engagement photos, or about the fact that the BMW they're leasing is costing them hundreds of pounds every month and putting them into debt. If your mindset is in the right place you won't feel the need to compare yourself to everyone else, because your 'why' – not someone else's 'why' – will be the driving force behind why you want what you want.

Warren Buffett made 99 per cent of all his money after the age of 52

This issue with comparison is especially important when it comes to your finances. Unlike what social media or the outside world might want to tell you, wealth is often built slowly, over the course of a person's life, and then passed down to future generations. You never know if the person sitting next to you at work was able to save up a house deposit because of the amount of money they're on, or because they got help from their parents or grandparents – but I'm willing to say that it's probably the latter. No disrespect to anyone who's received help – I'm all about building and passing down generational wealth – but don't compare your Day 1 to someone else's Day 100. Run your own race. Warren Buffett, one of the most accomplished and famous investors of our time, is a 91-year-old multi-billionaire today, but he actually built over 90 per cent of his wealth after he was 65 years-old. He would not have been able to achieve that had he not spent the first two-thirds of his life learning and building good financial habits.

'I'm 35 and I'm still living at home with my parents, I'm a failure'

When advising clients or speaking to people at events, I'll hear things like this. But I couldn't disagree more. Being a failure isn't about the situation you find yourself in, it's an attitude – a mindset – and I make sure to say this to them. From my perspective, if you're 35 and you're living at home with your parents, this means that you can probably save a lot more money than someone who is renting, you are spending time with your family and helping around the house, and if the worst were to happen and you were to lose your job, you could still keep a roof over your head while you look for another one.

Meanwhile, the people you are comparing yourself to – the 20-something-year-olds who have just got on the housing ladder – may have burnt through all of their savings just to come up with a deposit, bought a flat in a poor location above market value, and on top of that may have a mortgage so big that they will spend the rest of their lives paying it off. It may sound like an extreme example, but these things happen. You've got to be very careful about the stories you tell yourself.

Footballer Ian Wright is a legend whom everybody knows and loves today, but he started his football career relatively late. Despite trialling for Southend United and Brighton & Hove Albion as a teenager, he did not get a contract offer from either team and instead spent his late teens and early twenties playing amateur football. He didn't go on to be signed to Crystal Palace until he was 22, which is old in football terms. Moral of the story: comparison is the thief of joy. Whatever is for you, will be for you.

Comparison can be useful

Comparison isn't always bad, though. If you're comparing yourself with others to arm yourself with information or for benchmarking purposes, this is absolutely fine, and in some cases it's necessary. Let's say you're working for a company and you've been in the same role for a while. The company hires someone at your level, you become friends with them, and you find out that they are being paid more than you to do the same job. The response to this is not to take it out on your colleague – they have done you a favour by providing you with very useful information. It's an opportunity for you to go and speak to your boss and make a case for why you deserve a pay rise based on the knowledge that you now have. If we don't do this in our places of work, pay gaps emerge, and we know that these are more likely to affect women, ethnic minorities, the disabled and other marginalised groups. So if you're trying to get somewhere financially, gather the data you need, but don't judge it. Use it to better your situation and move forward.

Keep your costs low; avoid lifestyle inflation

Once we stop playing the comparison game, we can begin to adopt financial habits which will serve us for years to come.

There are three habits I would like to recommend. I call them habits to live by. The first financial habit to live by is to keep your costs low and avoid lifestyle inflation. If you've never heard of lifestyle inflation, this is when a person's expenses always rise to meet their income, no matter how much they are paid. It's a very easy habit to fall into. You start a job in a low-paying role, and you feel financially restricted because of how much money you are earning. Then one day – congratulations – you get a pay rise. Finally you can buy those Yeezys or that Chanel bag you've been eyeing up. Maybe you upgrade your car or move into a bigger house or flat.

Habit 1 – beware of lifestyle creep: the future is not guaranteed

It might feel good getting all these new shiny things, but let me tell you something: if your expenses match your income 100 per cent, this is a sure-fire way to run into financial difficulty. Why? Because the future is not guaranteed. When I got made redundant in 2019, it came out of nowhere. I thought I was doing well at my job and I had no idea that my employer would be cutting staff. Thank goodness I'd got into the habit of putting aside a portion of my income every month so that I had an emergency fund when that happened. If I hadn't had my own savings to rely on, that would have been a much more stressful time for me and my family. If you can, create a lifestyle that you are happy with across all your needs and wants, and the next time you get a pay rise, rather than use it to spend on more stuff, use it to save or invest. We will cover saving and investing in Chapters 11 and 13. This is an essential component of the wealth-building process. Get yourself to a lifestyle that you are happy and content with – both your needs and your wants – and then dramatically increase your income above this amount by saving and investing your extra money. People who do this are the complete opposite of those who increase their expenses every time they get a pay rise. People who do this become wealthy.

Habit 2 – develop multiple streams of income

A second financial habit to live by is not to rely on one stream of income. Like not spending everything you earn and falling into lifestyle creep, this is another way to minimise financial risk. If I am going to be real with you, yes, you may get on with the people at your job, and yes, you might have a great relationship with your line manager, but at the end of the day, if you work for a company, you are a cost to that company and they will let you go if the survival of the business depends on it. Same way, if you were to drop down dead today – heaven forbid – the people at your company would mourn you, would send flowers to your family, but they would also advertise your job the very next day. So you've got to back yourself.

This might sound like cold behaviour by companies, but in exactly the same way that you would stop paying your gym membership if it was putting too much pressure on your finances, your company would let you go if you or a group of staff were too much of a cost to them. Every so often you read a news story about how a large company closes down one of its business divisions, in some cases letting go of hundreds of members of staff in the process. If you've been saving a percentage of your money each month this will enable you to get through an emergency, but if you want to move forward you're still going to have to earn. This is why I encourage everyone I speak to to bring in at least two streams of income. This means that if you lose one stream, you can still rely on the second. How many streams of income should you have? Well, according to the Internal Revenue Service in the United States, most millionaires have seven income streams. I'm not telling you to run out and get seven; this is just to give you an idea of how people are earning money at the highest level.

So how can you get started earning extra income streams? We're going to talk about building a side hustle in Chapter 6, so make sure you read it, but the key message I'd like to share here is to start with what you have. So if you work for a marketing company, for example, see if you can offer your marketing services to start-ups and small businesses in your local community or on social media. Yes, there may be some clauses in your contract which say that you can't work with certain clients and so on, but an increasing number of employers understand the need for their staff to have financial security. You just have to be upfront and honest with them, and not get rumbled on social media for building a six-figure competitor brand! Another thing to bear in mind with multiple streams of income is that you don't necessarily need to double your income. Let's use £1,000 as an example income; there are many different ways in which you can bring home £1,000 a month. This could be £1,000 from a nine-to-five job; £500 from a nine-to-five and £500 from a side hustle; or it could be

£500 from a nine-to-five, £250 from a side hustle and £250 from rental income. As Gary Vaynerchuk says, 'How you make your money is more important than how much you make.'

Habit 3 – build an emergency fund

The third and final financial habit to live by is to have an emergency fund. Again, this continues the theme of making sure that you have money to spare. An emergency fund – or, as some people like to call it, a rainy-day fund – is a store of cash that you set aside in case you lose your job or have to make a large, unexpected purchase. I know that the idea of saving money just to have it there might seem a little strange, but, as we have already discussed, life isn't guaranteed, and you never know when your fridge might break down, your car might need a replacement part, or you end up stranded on holiday with no way to get back home. You get the point. The whole idea of an emergency fund is that you save enough money to last you for a set amount of time, depending on what your level of expenses is. I recommend having an emergency fund to cover three to six months, as this is the amount of time during which you might have to make ends meet after, for example, losing your job, giving you enough time to apply for and start a brand-new position. So if your monthly expenses cost you £2,000 a month, then a three-month emergency fund would be – you guessed it – £6,000. Does three to six months' expenses sound too much? That's absolutely fine; even having a lump sum of £500 or £1,000 put away is better than having nothing. No one is expecting you to save the full three to six months' worth straight away. As with everything else when it comes to money, you can start with what you have and then build.

Another thing I advise is to have an emergency credit card. A low or 0 per cent interest credit card with a high credit limit, if used sensibly, can be a very useful tool if you find yourself in an emergency situation. A credit card will give you fast and quick access to money if, for example, you find yourself stranded on holiday with no cash, or if you need to make a really big one-off purchase.

So there are my three financial habits to live by. I hope you take them on board and put them into practice. I trust they will serve you as well as they've served me.

Let me tell you a story about comparison

Meet Vanessa. Vanessa's doing OK – she went to uni, studied hard and has a decent job. She's just got a promotion and she now earns £60k a year. But even though she's doing well, she continues to compare herself to other people, and because of that she feels like a failure. She has friends who are earning more than her, friends who are earning less than her but seem to be 'living their best life', and friends who run businesses. One of her friends is a hairdresser, and so is able to charge clients what she likes and book her own time off to go on holiday. Meanwhile Vanessa feels like she's stuck at a computer from nine to five, working.

So even though she's made it to £60k, which is well above what the average person earns in the UK, she's forever down on herself. Her friends all rent their own apartments but she still lives at home. Her friends drive BMWs and Mercedes, she drives a Vauxhall Corsa. So she starts to use credit cards, taking her friends out to expensive dinners and going on holidays. Rather than fly standard-class, which she can afford, she pays for business-class. And again, she has to use overdrafts and loans to be able to manage her lifestyle.

And this all leads to her getting herself into a huge amount of debt which she can no longer afford. The letters coming through the post asking for payment, the daily calls from the different companies she owes money to leave her stressed and unable to sleep without taking sleeping pills. Struggling to pay her debt, Vanessa decides to get an Individual Voluntary Arrangement – an IVA – which is basically a five- to six-year debt repayment plan that people enter into when they can't afford to pay off their debts. The IVA means Vanessa can no longer get credit and has to live on cash, and so she learns to live within her means. Finally, when she comes off the IVA, she promises herself never to put herself in that situation again. She no longer compares herself to other people. She focuses on ways in which she can build up her income and make more money. Unfortunately, because she has had to get an IVA, it has affected her credit file – her credit history – and so she has limited access to credit, but she chooses to see this as a positive as she would rather avoid credit for the time being anyway.

My message to you is: don't be like Vanessa. There's no need for you to compare yourself to other people. Wherever you are in life right now, you're doing great. Run your own race and build slowly.

5

Working a Nine-to-Five

This chapter is about working a nine-to-five, how to look for a job, get a job and keep a job. Don't let those social media business 'gurus' fool you: there is nothing wrong with working a job. According to the Office for National Statistics, there were 32.5 million people aged 16 years and over in employment between September and November 2020, nearly two-thirds of the adult population. So for most of us, getting a regular job is going to be a primary source of income. There is a big debate online – mainly brought up by social media entrepreneurs posing beside jets and sitting on the bonnets of Lamborghinis – as to whether if you work a job, you are in some way inferior to someone who runs a business. Let me tell it to you straight – income is income. A job provides a great way for you to earn a steady income, pay into a pension, learn the ins and outs of your industry and build a network. I might run my own business today, but the only reason why I've been able to build everything I have is because of what I learnt working as a financial adviser. So the structure of this chapter is going to be super-simple. I'm going to give you my top ten tips for working a nine-to-five. They are all things I have used in my career, and if you put them into practice they will work well in yours.

TIP 1 Be punctual

It's very important for you to be on time in any job you work – and for that matter, anything you do in life. I don't want to hear about African time and Black-man timing (commonly abbreviated to BMT, for those who are unfamiliar). There is a famous saying that goes, 'If you're on time, you're late.' You need to live by this saying. If you work at a company that has a Monday morning meeting at 9 a.m., you don't want to be the person running into the meeting room at 9:02 a.m., breathing heavily and saying, 'The Tube was on strike.' Your boss, who takes the same Tube to work as you do, knows that you over-slept. If you have to be somewhere at 9 a.m., aim to be there at 8:45 a.m. This way you have time to get settled, make a coffee and prepare for the meeting.

A big reason why people get promoted at work is because they are trusted by those in charge to take on additional responsibilities. Would you rely on a takeaway service if the food constantly showed up at your door late? If you can demonstrate that you are punctual, that means you are dependable. Management will be like, 'Let's ask Mary to open up, Mary will be there.' Before you know it, you've taken on some extra responsibility – and boom, a few months later you can make the case for why you deserve a promotion and a pay rise.

It's that simple. If you struggle with punctuality, plan your journey in advance; Google Maps is your friend. Work out the best route to get to where you need to go, and even put the time of your journey in your calendar or planner if you have to. And don't forget the famous saying, 'The early bird catches the worm.' To wake up early, you need to go to bed early. So have a cut-off time when you put your phone down and turn off the TV. Yes, I know you want to watch the latest episode of *Love Island*. You can always record it and watch it in your own time.

TIP 2 Focus on progression

Whatever role you're in, you want to be constantly asking yourself, 'What's the next step?' Your company isn't just going to promote you because you've worked there the longest. You need to take responsibility for your own career and find out from your employer how you can rise up through the company – employers really like this. So it's important to get mentorship, and find out from the people who are more senior to you how you can progress in the way they have. A good idea is to speak to your team lead or manager and find out how they got to the role they are in today. Offer to take them out for coffee. You'll be surprised by how keen people are to talk about their achievements! Once they've told you what they did, you can emulate the bits that apply to you in your own career. As US motivational speaker Tony Robbins once said, 'Success leaves clues.'

Another top tip is for you to find the job description of the next job you want, then look for opportunities to gain that experience. Remember that in a place of work you are rarely paid for what you say you're going to do; you're paid for what you've already done. So look at job listings that your company might be putting out, or look at job descriptions for companies in a similar industry to yours. What are employers asking prospective candidates to do at the job level you're aiming for? Make a note of all the things you're currently doing and pay attention to the gaps in your experience, then ask for opportunities to do or shadow this kind of work in your company. Now, you might have to work outside normal working hours, or do some extra-curricular activity to gain this experience, but once you get that promotion it's yours to keep, and all the effort will have been worth it.

TIP 3 Your network is your net worth

It's very important that you network both inside and outside your work. What do I mean by inside and outside work? I'll explain – starting with networking 'inside' where you work. When I worked as a financial adviser, I had a legal requirement to write reports to submit to my clients. Writing wasn't really my strong suit back then, so I made the decision to reach out to someone on the compliance team and ask for their help with report-writing. I don't drink and I don't smoke, but in the process of networking with compliance I would offer to take them out to a bar or the pub and have a chat. I had to take myself out of my comfort zone to better myself and my career. And guess what? They were happy to share their report-writing tips with me in exchange for a drink after work, and I completed all my reports to a great standard.

Now, by networking outside work I mean networking within your industry to become a household name within your sector. If you are well known within your industry because of the work you do, I can guarantee that you will be an asset to your company. Back in the day, you would have to go to events and conferences to be able to do this. Don't get me wrong, there's still a place for in-person events, but there's an even easier way to network within your industry, and that's by using LinkedIn. I promise you that if you exchange the amount of time you spend on social media with time spent on LinkedIn, you will be able to raise your business profile. Not only that, but you will raise your company's profile; and when the time comes for someone to be put on a particular project or be sent overseas to give a presentation about the company, you will be the one chosen.

TIP 4 Find a mentor

Take it from me, a smart person learns from other people's mistakes as well as their successes. If you want to level up your career, you need to get yourself a mentor. A mentor doesn't need to be someone you know that well, and contrary to what you might think they don't need to be older than you either. I've had mentorship from many people who are younger than me. A mentor just needs to be someone you can look up to and who has gone where you want to go. Mentors are great because they can advise you in a matter of minutes on things that it might take you days, weeks or even months to work out on your own. Mentors can also hold you accountable, so if you set yourself a bunch of targets you can be sure that your mentor is going to check in with you about your progress, or lack thereof.

How do you find a mentor? Personal introductions are great, so start with the people you know and find out if there is someone in your network with the skills and expertise to help you. But also consider using – you guessed it – LinkedIn! I love it when I see proactive people on LinkedIn posting about their skills and aspirations and asking if their connections know someone who can help them. If you don't ask, you don't get. It's important when looking for a mentor to think not only about what they can offer you, but what you are offering them. Some mentors just want to give someone a helping hand because someone else helped them. Other mentors might be interested in some of the connections you have, or might want to learn more about your skills or your industry. A final thing to consider is paying for mentorship. Paying for mentorship can cost a lot of money, but it can be worth its weight in gold if you connect with the right person. If you are early on in your career and don't have the money, then you may be able to find a mentor who is willing to work with you pro bono. But if you're working with someone who has a track record of positive results through their mentoring, leave yourself open to paying a fee, especially if their mentorship is helping you to increase your income.

TIP 5   Interview well

Many people dread job interviews, but for me they are one of the most exciting parts of the application process. Along with your CV, interviews are a way for you to put on your sharpest clothes, your power shoes and show a prospective employer what you're made of. The main skill you'll be using in interviews is public speaking, which explains the 'dread' part. I know some people who would rather fight a bear than have to speak publicly. But public speaking is a skill, and as with any skill you can improve your confidence with practice. I haven't always been the outgoing, outspoken person I am today. Back when I wanted to level up my public speaking, I did drama lessons. It was during these lessons that I learnt the importance of creating a persona. You see musicians do this all the time. When Rihanna is on stage she is acting out a persona she created to perform her music, but in her day-to-day life she's Robyn Fenty. This is an important psychological tool you can use in your next interview.

Another important point when it comes to interviews is that preparation is key. When you see a performer on stage, rarely will they be speaking off the dome. Whether it's a musician, comedian, politician or actor, the stuff you see them saying has been rehearsed hundreds of times. All you see is the end result. So have in mind what you want to say ahead of your interview, and also have in your back pocket any potential unexpected questions they could ask you on the day. You can search the internet for commonly asked interview questions online and their recommended responses, and make them your own. You will never have to draw a blank at the 'What are your salary expectations?' question. Also, I can't not mention LinkedIn yet again. You can used LinkedIn to research the people who will be interviewing you, so you will have questions ready to ask them when they ask you the inevitable 'Any questions for us?' Hint – always say 'yes'.

TIP 6   Big yourself up on your CV

Like a job interview, your CV is a prime opportunity for you to brag about your achievements. At the CV stage of recruitment, the people hiring won't necessarily know who you are yet, so don't be afraid to boast. I think people are too humble when it comes to CVs. They think a CV is supposed to be a factual retelling of your work history. But what about your achievements? What's one thing you were able to change in your organisation or bring to your role? What did you implement? Make sure to talk about the things you did above and beyond your role as well. And make sure to spell out the results. So if you created a new bookings system for an events company, talk about how much time or money it saved.

Once you've done your first draft, get someone else to read your CV. You can go on – hello again! – LinkedIn and find a recruiter or manager and ask them for feedback. Send your CV to a friend, family member or partner to check for spelling mistakes and typos. And when you finally send your CV in, accompany it with a cover letter to the hiring manager and connect with them. I know people who have done this who have ended up with a higher job offer than what they initially applied for, just because they were able to build a rapport with the people doing the hiring.

TIP 7   Be strategic

A well-paid job that you want, in an industry you want, is very unlikely to fall into your lap. If you want to get a job that's right for you, you're going to have to be intentional. There is a point at the start of everyone's career when you will need to work simply to build up your skills and experience. But the more companies you work for, the more intentional you'll need to be when seeking new roles. For example, a great way to be intentional is to research the salaries for certain job roles before deciding where to apply. Glassdoor and PayScale are two great websites you can use to find out the salaries of job roles in the UK. Employees and former employees of companies can share their pay anonymously on these websites, which is great information to have to hand while doing your research.

Also remember that not all industries are created equal, and neither are the different regions of the UK. Technology and finance are, unsurprisingly, two of the highest-paid industries in the UK, compared to retail and hospitality jobs. Companies in London tend to pay higher salaries on average than companies in the north-east. Ideally there would be more of a balance between the various sectors and locations in the UK, and maybe one day we'll get there; but the reality is that this just isn't the case. This is why, if you would like to increase your income, you are sometimes required to do something a bit different, even if it means pushing yourself out of your comfort zone. Use the internet to your advantage and if need be follow the money.

TIP 8 Negotiate your salary

Once your CV is accepted and you've aced your interview, don't forget to negotiate your salary. I know of people who have ended up on two wildly different salaries for similar roles because one of them chose to negotiate before accepting the job and the other did not. Negotiating your salary doesn't only have to happen at the moment you get hired, though; you should also be having regular pay reviews with your manager and setting goals with them, which when completed, you can go back to your manager with and use as evidence as to why you deserve a promotion. This will enable you to progress to the next level. By researching the average salaries for the roles you're interested in you will be able to offer a number that makes sense when you are asked about your salary expectations. Hint: it's generally a safe bet to ask for an amount that is just below the maximum salary for the role. It gives you space to progress if you are accepted for the job.

You also have to be willing to turn down opportunities or go elsewhere. You need to be willing to turn down a job that you've applied for if the salary is not enough to justify leaving your previous position. Also, if you are looking for a promotion, you must be willing to move elsewhere if your current job will not or cannot increase your pay further. You typically get paid more when you leave and start at a new company than when you get promoted internally. In this day and age there is no such thing as a job for life. Just make sure that if you are going to turn down a position or move on to a different company, you definitely have an alternative and are not leaving yourself without a job.

TIP 9 Get to know your payslip

If you're one of those people who never reads their payslip unless they've had a promotion – stop it! You should be checking your payslip every month. Not just to see what your take-home pay is, but also all the deductions and benefits that are removed and added to your payslip every month. As we all know, there's no such thing as receiving 100 per cent of your salary. Every month you pay Income Tax, National Insurance, contribute to a pension and pay off a portion of your student loan. You should be as familiar with all these monthly deductions as you were with your net pay, because sometimes mistakes happen. Sometimes you might be given an emergency tax code, or it might be wrong altogether, in which case you should be due a tax refund from HMRC. You might get a pay increase, or the government might change the tax rules, which could push you into a different tax bracket. You won't know what to look out for if you don't familiarise yourself with your payslip. The simplest way to make sure you are paying roughly the correct amount of deductions is to use a salary tax calculator online. There are a number of different websites where you can put in your annual salary, your level of pension contributions and the year you went to university, and they will calculate how much all your deductions should amount to. Be sure to make use of these free tools.

You may be receiving benefits from your job, too. Some companies will pay you a car allowance, or invest a portion of your salary into a company stock purchase plan. Other companies will give you an advance on a bicycle or train ticket which you can then pay back to the company in instalments. You should be checking your payslip for all these too. If you don't understand anything in your payslip, speak to your HR department, and they will be able to explain what the various numbers and codes on it mean.

TIP 10   Understand your contract

I know how it is. You apply for a job and they send you a bunch of paperwork to read though and sign. Your pension documents, the staff handbook, your contract. Normally the longest and most complicated of these documents is your contract, which is precisely why you should take the time to read through it properly. Your contract will include your salary, the terms around your probation and notice period, the work you'll be expected to do, the company disciplinary process and the flexible working policies. How does your job feel about you running a side hustle? Working for competitors? Posting on social media? Make sure you find where all this information is, and if you are unsure ask someone you trust to be a second pair of eyes and look over it for you.

If there are any benefits or specifics that you discussed in your interview, make sure that they are written into your contract. Every so often I hear a story about someone who was promised heaven and earth at interview but didn't get it when they started because it was never agreed in writing. And remember your contract is a two-way document – it's as much about what you are promising to do for your company as what they are promising to do for you as their employee.

Let me tell you a story about working a nine-to-five

I used to work in banking, and to be very honest with you – I loved it. I loved the security. I loved working with and being part of a team, making friends and networking with people.

But the one thing I realised is that having a nine-to-five meant that my aspirations were never the priority. I always had to fit into the work. My job never tried to work around me, I always had to work around my job. An example of this is that if I ever felt sick, I'd have to call in the morning before a certain time. If my train was delayed, I'd have to take pictures to prove it or I could get into trouble. But, on the other hand, if I was ever paid late or there was a mistake on the payroll there wouldn't be that same urgency from the other side. So I'd have to check my payslip to make sure I was getting paid the right amount.

I remember not being able to take holidays when other people went off. And it used to be so frustrating, forever having to dance to somebody else's tune. Ultimately, what really affected me and changed me was being made redundant. I got made redundant three times. The third time, I'd taken time off after having my fourth child, was on paternity leave for two weeks, came back and they sacked me. They sacked me with a two-week-old child and three other children.

That was the point in my life where I was like, 'I'm not going back.' Many of us either have had or will have that not going back moment. You have that moment where you say, 'You know what, I'm not going to allow somebody else to put me in this position.' So I worked on my side hustle evenings and weekends, and I continued to build until I started to do it full-time.

This started in March 2019. I created a lot of content on social media, I was doing Instagram lives weekly to build a relationship with my audience, I appeared on other people's platforms and added a great deal of value, I gave talks and held workshops. I was extremely focused and driven. By August 2019, I'd done so much content and got my name out there to such an extent that I had the opportunity to appear on my first television show. And I haven't looked back since.

Don't get me wrong; having a nine-to-five is great. A job can give you the stability you need. But what also counts is what you're doing from five to nine. That's what's going to change your life. What you do from nine to five is going to keep you alive, keep you where you're at and help you pay your bills. But it's what you do from five till nine that's really going to give you a different life to everyone else.

6

Running a Business/ Setting up a Side Hustle

Business is an exchange of value

In this chapter we're going to talk about how to create a business. As we all know, it's not enough to have just one source of income, and creating a business is a great way to build additional income streams. Setting up a business is not the same as setting up a limited company, designing a logo and getting business cards made. Why are you giving yourself limited company admin when you have no sales? You have a business once you can create value for others and start selling. Then, once you start to make sales, you can create a limited company.

Every time you spend money on something, that's someone else's business. The reason why you are happy to pay them is because they have created value in your life. Everything from the Deliveroo you ordered last week, when you couldn't be bothered to cook, to the gas and electricity you use to heat and power your home. In the same way that you are happy to pay for value, other people are happy to pay you for that same value. Once you see the exchange of money as an exchange of value, it will completely change your life.

The difference between a business and a side hustle

There's also a difference between being self-employed and being an entrepreneur. A small business owner, on the other hand, hires other people based upon a product or service. Entrepreneurship is about scale – nationally, geographically – and your business doesn't require you to be in it every single day. You have been able to replicate yourself to other people so they can perform those roles.

People don't respect hustles. I know people who buy trainers, paintings and so on from discounted stores and sell them online and make money. E-commerce is something that so many of us are not doing; why haven't more of us thought about selling products on Amazon? You don't even have to hold the stock any more now that there's drop shipping.

Your business starts inside you

So how do you create a valuable business? Well, the place your business starts is inside you. These days everyone wants to build an app. Whenever I talk to someone who wants to do so, I already know they aren't serious about building a business because they're just creating a business they think they're supposed to create. You're not going to be the next Mark

Zuckerberg – that ship has sailed. But you could be the next pioneer in your field if you focus on your unique skills and talents. To create a business you need to have or learn a skill which someone is willing to pay for. Once you have that, you have a business. If you don't have any skills – which I really doubt is the case, because everyone has something to offer – then you need to find a mentor to teach you. So what are you passionate about? What are you good at? Whether it's cooking, project management or graphic design, start there.

Finding your target audience

Many people might not know this, but when I started my business (which was called Noir Excel at the time), I started in the church. In business, the warmest leads are the easiest to convert into customers. Warm leads include people who you already know and have a connection with, people who are actively seeking your product, and people who need your product. It just so happened that, for me, the warmest leads in my life were the people I went to church with every week. It also goes without saying that the colder the lead, the harder they are to convert. Cold leads are people you do not have an existing relationship with, people who are not actively seeking your product, and people who need to be educated as to how your product might help them.

The people at my church sat somewhere in the middle: they were people I knew well and had good relationships with, but they did not know they were in need of financial education. So I ran free financial education seminars and workshops at the church, delivering as much value as I could at these sessions, and when people started to reach out to me, I was able to offer them my financial advisory services. There is still a place for offline marketing if the leads are there, but once I found I'd exhausted all my leads at my church, I took my business online. We cannot, of course, talk about business marketing without talking about social media.

Social media marketing

Just a few decades ago, if you wanted to market your business to new audiences and expand your reach it might have meant advertising your business in the local newspaper or on the community notice board. But today one of the easiest ways to market your business, for free, is on social media. Social media is used by millions of people all over the world every single day. So we cannot underestimate it as a lead generation tool. If you run a product-based business, you can use social media to post appealing pictures of your product, with a clear link to where people can buy it. If you run a service-based business, you can post explainer videos of your service and the problems it solves for your customers. If your videos are useful, this will be reflected in your engagement: your likes, comments, shares and DMs – and this is what leads to sales.

How I got started on social media

I started creating social media content in 2017 soon after I stopped running financial education workshops at my church. I developed a brand of witty, straight-talking financial education videos explaining how money works, and talking about issues I knew affected my community. Videos like 'Have you eaten your house deposit?' were a hit with my community because I knew I was speaking to people who had self-confessed takeaway habits, but also had larger aspirations to build wealth. There weren't many people doing what I did back then, and my status as a qualified financial adviser gave me the credibility to speak on financial issues. Today, my social media content has led to broadcasting opportunities, business partnerships and introductions to thousands of people I have never met. I don't say this to brag, only to demonstrate to you the power of social media marketing. While my business was about financial education, I do believe you can create a business about practically anything. The internet has given us unparalleled access to customers all over the world, for a relatively low cost. Use it!

The power of word of mouth

Word of mouth has also been a very powerful tool for me in my business journey. Let me ask you a question: would you be more likely to buy from a business because of what it says about itself, or based upon what other people say about it? If you picked the latter, I completely agree with you. Word of mouth is an extremely powerful way to build trust in your business, which is why whenever you buy something from Amazon or order a takeaway, you normally get a request afterwards to review what you've just bought. Something I did very early on was to offer my financial education seminars for free and then ask for feedback and testimonials. I then shared those testimonials publicly, on my website and on social media. People are way more likely to buy from you if you have social proof, so don't feel shy about asking for feedback whenever someone transacts with you. Make sure also to accept all the feedback that's given to you, good and bad. If you get a negative testimonial, take the feedback on board and use it to improve your service. If someone has taken the time to let you know how to make your product better, listen to them!

Why do you want to run a business?

On the subject of business, we must again come back to the principle of 'knowing your "why"'. If you are trying to create a business from a place of vanity, it isn't likely to last very long. Your reason for wanting to create a business needs to be bigger than getting likes on social media, or being able to put 'entrepreneur' in your bio. I'll let you know why I wanted to create a business: because I wanted to be financially free. After my experience of being made redundant and having spoken to many people who had faced similar circumstances, I needed to know that how I fed and took care of my family was in my hands. All too often, your financial destiny is in the hands of somebody else. You need to be able to feed and protect your family.

Some people have a calling or an idea so great that they can't stop thinking about it. Others may be experiencing issues either personally or in their local community which they feel the need to improve. You might have heard of an online scheduling tool called Calendly, which you can use to book meetings with people by sharing available slots in your calendar. What you might not know is that the founder and

CEO of that business is a Nigerian-American man called Tope Awotona, who grew tired of the constant back and forth of emails when trying to book in meetings with clients and colleagues. Whatever your reason, if you know your 'why' you can go extremely far.

Building a business requires work

There's knowing why you want to run a business and then there's actually building a business. After many years in this game, I've got to say to you that building a business requires hard work. No one lived a nice life without hard work. Work is required even if you want the softest life possible. This doesn't mean you need to work every hour under the sun, and it also doesn't mean not working smart. But in reality it does mean that if you are working a nine-to-five, you will probably have to use your evenings, weekends and perhaps even some of your annual leave to get your business off the ground and start building some traction. Anyone who says it's possible to build a business without putting in the hours is probably trying to sell you something or is getting help from someone else. If building a successful business was that easy, then everyone would have one.

Approach business with an abundance mindset

A lot of us don't want to start a business because we don't think it's possible to make money outside of a nine-to-five. What I say is, people need to have an abundance mindset, not a scarcity mindset. There is money to be made every single day of the week. You just need to work out how you're going to access a particular income stream and how you're going to take the money out. You could go with your hands, or a bucket, or you could build a pipe so you can access this stream whenever you want to. But the point is, try not to limit yourself. You may have been raised to think that you need to work for someone else your whole life, but there's more to life than that. I'm here to encourage you to dream a bit bigger. The same way you are willing to pay money for value in your life, other people will be willing to pay you money for that same value. So back yourself. Develop your skills if you need to, be prepared to put the work in, and you will be rewarded.

Working a nine-to-five vs being an entrepreneur

Let me make it very clear. When it comes to working a nine-to-five vs being an entrepreneur, I am not saying that one is better than the other. You often see this debate come up on social media that running a business is somehow superior to working a nine-to-five, and I don't believe that at all. If you're working a job, paying your bills and supporting your family, you are doing great. You can be paid very well in a high-paying job, and you can struggle to make ends meet in a nine-to-five. But I can't talk to you about creating wealth and increasing your income without discussing running a business, because it's such a powerful wealth creation tool. Myself and my wife, we do both. I run a business and she has a job. This gives us the stability of her regular pay cheque and the uncapped income potential of the family business. This set-up works for us. Even I, if I am offered a nine-to-five job and it's right for me, I am going to collect that cheque. Being an entrepreneur isn't a religion. I am happy to dip in and out of doing a nine-to-five, but I will never rely on a single source of income.

Let me tell you a story about business

I think the hardest thing when it comes to running a business or a side hustle is staying focused and motivated. Unlike in a job, nobody's going to be on your case if you don't send an email, or if you oversleep and turn up to work late. It's all on you. In a job there are systems and processes set up to make sure things get done. You get regular reviews from your manager, if you've got expenses you submit them and somebody else pays. But when you go self-employed, if you don't set your alarm and you don't wake up, nothing gets done. And in business, when nothing gets done you don't make money.

So it's really important for you to make sure that you focus. Treat your side hustle or business as you would your nine-to-five. Even more, I always tell people that if they are prepared to wake up at six or seven o'clock in the morning to go to somebody else's business, they should be prepared to wake up even earlier for their own. You should be able to – and want to – do more for yourself than you do working for others. So get yourself up, get the systems in place and have a routine to maximise your chances of success. Maybe you might want to work from a café or a local co-working space. I know these might be added expenses, but sometimes it feels good to get up and go somewhere else. There's nothing wrong with going into a shared space maybe once or twice a week, just so you have colleagues or other people to talk to in your working environment. These are all things you can do.

However, the biggest thing for me when it comes to building a business is to invest in yourself. Don't get me wrong: this can be very hard when you've got a job, a family or other responsibilities. In my household it's very tempting to just stop work when the kids get home from school at four o'clock, but sometimes you've got to keep going. I worked far later than that when I had a nine-to-five, quite regularly.

I love running a business. I love the freedom it gives me. I love the fact that I don't have to miss my kids' sports days and that I can be an active father and husband. I can support my wife in what she needs to do. Running a business has a lot of pros, but it also has some cons. I always tell people that for the first three years of having my own business, I could have made more money employed than as self-employed But now, after five years, I make three to four times what I used to make when I was employed. A business takes a while to build up, but once you've done it the sky is the limit.

7

Budgeting

In this chapter we're going to talk about budgeting. I know, I know, whenever you hear the word 'budget' your mind wants to go to sleep. I can already hear you snoring as I write this! But no matter what you call it, whether it's a budget, a spending plan or a money diary, you need to have an idea of where your money is coming from. This is one of the most – if not *the* most – important principles of money management. If you don't know how much money you've got coming in or going out, it doesn't matter how much money you make. If your expenses are more than your income, that is a recipe for ending up with no money. And with money – as with many things in life – if you want to be able to do the so-called 'exciting' stuff, like investing and so on, you've got to master the basics. Budgeting is a great place to start.

I'd like to quickly mention the 50/30/20 principle. This is a budgeting method that says you should allocate 50 per cent of your expenses to your needs, 30 per cent to your wants and 20 per cent to savings. I don't think there is anything wrong with this budgeting method per se, but I do realise that a 20 per cent savings rate is a lot for many people, and also that a lot of people's needs might be running at more than 50 per cent of their monthly income. In my opinion, percentages like these should be used as a general guide and applied to your specific situation.

You've got to know where your money is coming from

How much money do you have coming in on a monthly basis? You'll be surprised how many people I ask and how many of my clients don't know the answer to this question. When their payslips get handed out or emailed to them at the end of the month, many people leave the email unread or hide the payslip at the bottom of a drawer, only to fish it out if they receive a pay rise, or get asked by a financial or mortgage adviser to produce their last six months of payslips. As I stressed in Chapter 5, you should be reading your payslip every month. Not just your payslip, but you should also be keeping a record of all your income. This includes any cashback you earn, any money you make from side hustles, selling stuff online, or any gifts or transfers. It is only once you have a complete picture of how much you have to work with month to month that you can make decisions about your spending.

Knowing your pay

A very common error I see people make is to mistake gross pay for net pay. I always point out that there's no such thing as taking home 100 per cent of your income. The taxman will always take his cut. A lot of people don't realise that if you are lucky enough to earn £120,000 a year, you don't take home £10,000 a month: after all the different deductions – Income Tax, National Insurance, student loan and pension contributions – the figure will be closer to £6,000 per month. It's not enough to know how much you earn in gross terms; you also need to realise how much will be hitting your bank account after deductions. This is your net pay and it is the amount you need to be aware of for budgeting purposes. The same applies if your pay isn't fixed. If you are on a zero-hours contract or self-employed – which means that your pay fluctuates from month to month – then work out your average pay over the last twelve months. This will give you a sense of how much you make month to month if your pay isn't fixed.

Work out how much you're spending

Here's a question I like to ask people – 'How much does it cost to be you?' It's a serious one. When you take all your fixed expenses, like your rent or mortgage, bills and subscriptions, and add them to your day-to-day costs like eating out, buying clothes and seeing friends, how much money do you normally spend on a monthly basis? Again, the vast majority of people have no clue. Too many of us are going out to Hakkasan (a high-end restaurant in Mayfair, London), and tapping our contactless card on the terminal hoping it isn't declined. This is no way to live! I am not saying you should know how much you are spending every hour of the day – that would be an unsustainable way to live – but you should be keeping a record of how much money you spend on a monthly basis, so you have an idea of whether you're living within your means or overspending. We all have a tendency to want to sugar-coat the past, and it might not be that comfortable to admit that you spent hundreds of pounds on clothes, or ordered ten takeaways last month, but if you want to make changes to your spending then you need to acknowledge the reality of it. There are plenty of free budgeting apps you can use to work out how much you're spending on a month-to-month basis and they will work out the different categories for you too. Apps like Emma and Money Dashboard both work well. App-only banks like Monzo, Starling and Revolut also offer similar budgeting tools, as do a growing number of high street banks.

Work out your disposable income

Subtract your monthly outgoings – both fixed and variable – from your monthly income and what you're left with is your disposable income. This is the amount of money you have left after you have paid your fixed expenses and any other regular payments that come out of your bank account every month. You can use your disposable income for a number of different purposes, like going out and enjoying yourself, but don't forget to budget for other priorities – I will give a few examples. If you have any high-interest debt in the form of credit cards, loans or overdrafts, you should allocate some of your disposable income to preventing your interest costs from building up. Aim to make at least your minimum payments each month, but if you are really trying to chip away at it, pay back as much as you can afford. Saving is also a very important priority and should be factored into your budget. Whether you're putting aside an emergency fund for a rainy day or saving towards something special, include savings as a line in your budget and treat it as a payment you are making to yourself – your future self.

Make a record of your spending

Once you've worked out an accurate picture of your income and your spending, make a record of it either in a spreadsheet or in a notebook. This will make your spending a reality and help you to create an accurate picture of what's going on. Look at your past few months of spending. If your 'income' figure is consistently higher than your 'expenses' figure, then well done! This means you are living within your means and have cash left over at the end of the month which you can use to save, invest or give to causes you care about. If the opposite is true and you consistently have an 'expenses' figure that is higher than your 'income' figure, then this is a sign that you are spending more than you earn and that you might need to make some tweaks and adjustments. Consistently overspending leads to people going broke, ending up in debt or even bankrupt. Think of it as a leaky bathroom pipe: over a long period of time, the seemingly small drip-drip of water is enough to destroy flooring, brickwork and much worse. Personally, I would look at your income and spending and score it out of ten. The aim here isn't to chastise yourself – it's just a way to keep a record of where you're at so that you can benchmark against yourself in the future. If you really want to add some accountability to your budgeting routine, see if you can budget with someone else. I do my budget with my wife. It keeps us both accountable in terms of what we're spending as a couple and what we're spending on the kids. For you it might be a friend or a trusted partner, but doing this exercise on a regular basis could be the motivation you need to keep up a budgeting habit.

So you've looked at the numbers

So you've recorded the numbers either in a notebook or on a spreadsheet – what do you think? Are you surprised by the amount that you've been spending? Most people normally are, and there's nothing wrong with this, especially if you're doing a budget for the first time; see it as taking stock. Things aren't going to be perfect, you're just trying to work out what the situation is. Now that you have a picture of what your income and your spending is like, it's time to start making some adjustments to both. Let's talk about your spending first. I am not a big fan of cutting back on your expenses, because there are only so many dry Jacob's cream crackers a person can eat before life starts getting depressing, but also because the amount by which you can trim your expenses is capped. However, the amount by which you can increase your income is virtually unlimited. But we will start with expenses because there are simple things we could be all doing to keep down our costs.

Making tweaks to your spending

Here are some simple things you can do to reduce your spending. Firstly, do a thorough review of all your bills and subscriptions. Take the monthly cost of any bill or subscriptions you pay for and multiply it by twelve. That £10 a month gift box subscription which you barely get round to opening when it arrives is costing you £120 a year! If there are things you pay for on a regular basis that you actually use or which bring some happiness to your life, keep using them. But if you have subscriptions you no longer use, or didn't even know you had, it's time to get rid of them. This will automatically unlock money in your budget that you can use elsewhere.

Do you have any spending habits that you'd like to bring under control? Maybe you are spending a bit too much on takeaways, or shopping online more often than you should? Try and have a set day once a week or once a month when you are allowed to treat yourself and commit to spending money just on that day. This way, your weekly takeaway day can be Friday, or you can allow yourself to make one online shopping order on the weekend. By phrasing it as 'I get to have a takeaway on day X' rather than 'I am not allowed to have takeaways on days X, Y and Z', you make this rule you've set for yourself a positive thing rather than a punishment.

Lastly, if you want to have more control over how much you're spending then consider paying yourself a monthly allowance out of your income every month like a bill, and pay it into a separate bank account if you can. Bonus points if you withdraw this amount and spend it in cash: this will limit your temptation to overspend or dip into your savings. Many years ago, when I wanted to get a handle on my spending I used to withdraw it in cash and spend it in coins and notes. As the weeks go on, you will be surprised how your mind naturally adjusts to how much you have left, and if you do spend it all you know you will need to run a tight ship until your next allowance.

Making tweaks to your income

No budgeting exercise would be complete without coming up with a plan to increase your income. Let's say you've run the numbers and you realise that you are overspending by £100 every month, even after you have cut back as much as possible. This could prompt you to see if you can bring in an extra £100 from elsewhere to supplement your primary income. There are plenty of things you can do, from booking in a meeting with your line manager to talk about your career progression and the possibility of getting a pay rise, to seeing if you can set up a side hustle and sell a product or service for that extra £100. We discussed how to set up a side hustle and increase your income in Chapter 6, but it's important that you do a budget first so you can have a sense of how much additional income you need or want to bring in.

Let me tell you a story about how I budget

I haven't always been great at budgeting. I used to have all my money coming into one account, and I would pay my bills from that account. I paid most of them manually, which was a big mistake as I didn't understand the importance of automating my payments by using direct debits. I learnt to set up a direct debit for my credit card the hard way. I would always pay it off on the fifteenth of each month, but one month I got really busy and forgot; this led to me missing the payment. Because of this I received a late payment fine, my credit score went down and I got that annoying call from the credit card company asking me why I missed my payment and whether

I could afford to pay. It was this painful slap in the face that woke me up and motivated me never to want to receive one of those calls again. I needed to set up systems which enabled me to manage my money on autopilot.

Now I have split my accounts into three – one for fixed costs, one for spending and one for saving. From my fixed-cost account I pay bills such as mortgage/rent, gas, electricity and so on in the first five days of the month. This makes sure all my bills are paid and keeps my providers happy that I am paying on time. You can call up your service providers and change your direct debit dates. I have a spending account with which I put myself on a budget, meaning that I don't just spend everything after I pay my bills; so a £100 a week would be £400 a month. This should be the only card you use to pay for food, travel to work, fuel and so on. I love digital banking apps which tell you every time you spend money and easily let you see where your money is going. This helps me to control my spending. My third account is for savings. I have an easy-access savings account that I use to build up my emergency fund. Once I reach my emergency fund target the money is used to achieve financial goals such buying a property, investing in the stock market or my business. I make sure to save as close to payday as possible, at the start of the month rather than at the end. I do this via standing order, from my fixed-cost account.

These are the types of things you can do to automate your money and make your money work for you, putting it in places where you need it to be and keeping funds that you don't want to dip into out of your line of sight. When it comes to managing your money, using systems and automation will always beat willpower or trying to rely on your memory.

8

How to
Spend Money

You might be surprised that there is a chapter in this book on how to spend money. But I had to include it because many of the money issues I see people running into result from them losing control of their spending. We are constantly being advertised to, invited to social occasions with family and friends, and it's natural to want to be able to treat yourself every now and again. So gaining an understanding of how to spend money is very important. The main thing I am going to emphasise in this chapter is the importance of developing rules and systems which will help guide you when you spend. We are only human, so relying on our willpower to stop us from buying that next round of champers at the club, or on our memory to know when to pay our next electricity bill, isn't always going to end well. By using systems which dictate how, when and how much money you spend, you will set yourself up for success and gain control of your finances. In this chapter I'll share with you the tools I now use to help guide my spending.

Have different accounts for different purposes

How many bank accounts do you have? Do you have different accounts for different purposes or are you getting paid into, spending and saving from the same one? If you are working from just one account and you are struggling to control your spending, this could be part of the problem. Often people tell me that they can't stop dipping into their savings. They develop a savings habit, put money away every month, but then they get a marketing email from their favourite clothing site, or they're having a fancy dinner out and dip into their savings to fund it. This sort of behaviour is completely human. If the money is there, you are much more likely to spend it. Once I realised this, I decided to split my money into different accounts to reduce my temptation to spend. Think about it – you have never, ever dipped into your pension savings to buy a car, a new dress or a first-class return ticket to Dubai (I'm gonna keep mentioning Dubai until people stop going there). This is because most people's pensions are in a completely separate account for which they probably don't know the login details and which they cannot legally access until they are in their fifties. This is very much by design, so apply this same principle to yourself.

Use a specific bank account for your monthly payments

A system I like to use to stay on top of my bills and monthly payments is called automation. I have set up the payments to come out automatically, freeing me up from having to remember to do it myself. We are all busy, after all. The account I get paid into is also the account I use for my bills, subscriptions and any credit payments. This ensures that all my bills are paid on time. This bank account also gives me cashback on my bills, which is perfect as this is money that I would have spent anyway. I have also set up my monthly payments to come out at a similar time each month – all my payments are made between the fifth and the tenth of the month, meaning that by the final bill date I know that everything has been paid for – car payments, TV streaming, gas, electricity and so on. If you want to change the date of your direct debits you can normally do this by logging into your account online or giving the supplier a call. You can normally move the date of online subscriptions by cancelling the subscription and then resubscribing on the day you want the new monthly payments to start. A lot of people don't realise that you can automate your debt repayments as well. If you have a credit card, for example, you can ask your credit card provider to set up a direct debit from your main bank account to automatically make the minimum payment every month so that it's never late. If you want to be more disciplined with your credit card usage you can set up what's called a variable direct debit to clear the card in full. Use automation for your monthly payments and give yourself one less thing to remember.

Use a bank account for your monthly spending

The bank account I spend from is completely different to the one I get paid into. Every month I put myself on a budget and pay an amount into my spending account, as if it were a monthly bill. The beauty of this system is that once you have paid into your spending account it becomes much more difficult for you to go over-budget, because every time you check your balance it will let you know much you have to work with until the end of the month. And you will be surprised – your brain will do a pretty good job of adjusting to the amount of money you have left as the month goes on. My spending account card is also the only card that I carry with me or use for my mobile payments. This again ensures that I am not dipping into any of my other accounts. When I first started to take charge of my spending many years ago, I took this system even further and used to withdraw a sum every month and spend only in cash.

The value of spending in cash

If you would like to change the way you spend for the better and you are just starting out, I fully recommend spending with cash as a way to master self-control. Technology has completely changed the way we spend money. In my lifetime alone I have seen people go from counting out coins to get on the bus – to tapping their phones and smartwatches to travel on the Tube. I am not against cashless payments. Sticking with the public transport example, they have made getting on the bus much quicker. But there is an entire generation of people for whom money isn't a tangible thing, it's just a series of numbers on a screen. Going back to cash makes the money you are spending 'real'. You physically have to count out and hand over the coins and notes, and you have a very visible reminder of how much money there is left. There are a lot of restaurants and shops that have moved away from accepting payments in cash, but I hope this trend doesn't take over completely. No matter how advanced our technology becomes, I think there will always be a place for spending in physical cash. It's a great way to build up your self-discipline when it comes to spending. Try giving it a go.

Have a separate savings account

It's very important that you have a bank account that is specifically for saving. Most importantly because it reduces the chance that you will dip into your savings as part of your day-to-day spending. This relies less on willpower and more on setting up an account that you can't easily access, perhaps even deleting the app from your phone and keeping the login details somewhere where you can only find them if you really need to. Saving into a separate account is also important because there are specific types of accounts which will reward you for so doing, either by paying you interest rates or bonuses. We will cover the main account types in Chapter 11, but the general principle here is that by not using a savings account you could be missing out on savings income. You can automate payments into your savings account as well, by setting up a standing order – an instruction for one bank account to automatically send a payment to another account on a particular day of the month. Some bank accounts also refer to this as a 'scheduled payment', but they are essentially the same thing. By automating your savings on or around the day you get paid, much as you would a monthly bill, you will hardly even notice this additional amount of money coming out of your bank account.

Pay yourself first

You have probably heard the saying 'pay yourself first', but do you actually understand what it means? It isn't immediately obvious at first glance, so let's break it down. Let's say you have a nine-to-five job. When you get paid, your employer moves money from their bank account into your bank account. This money is now yours, forever, until you spend it on something. You will obviously need to spend some of this money on things you need – food, bills, housing, clothes and so on. But we live in a consumerist society, and so there are plenty of companies whose job it is to convince you to give the rest of your money to them. Everywhere you turn nowadays there are adverts – on public transport, on our social media feeds, on the radio and of course on TV. So your job is to make sure that whenever you get paid, before you send a single penny to anyone else, you first make a payment to yourself, in the form of a saving, in a separate savings account. A portion of all the money you earn should be yours to keep. Then you can give money to the electricity company or your local takeaway, which knows you so well that they don't even need to ask you what your order is any more. If you think about the fact that many of us will be paid hundreds of thousands of pounds over the course of our careers, even if you saved a very small percentage of that it would still amount to a substantial sum of money over the course of a lifetime.

Dealing with emotional spending

When it comes to emotional spending – I understand it. Trust me. This is coming from someone whose parents didn't have a lot of money and used to send me to school with black school trousers, black school shoes and thick white tennis socks. The kids at school used to tease me and ask me when The Jackson 5 was getting back together. So it was no surprise that I spent my entire childhood wishing I had more money, and that I wasn't the most responsible with money once I started to make it myself. I call experiences like these 'poverty scars', and I still have to keep my poverty scars in check today. Maybe you spend money when you're a bit down, or you feel like you have to spend money on other people so that they will like you. You need to develop an awareness of your emotional spending triggers and the times in your life when they are most likely to crop up. The triggers will be different for everyone, but having them is completely normal. So in response to my poverty scars, I've had to change my mindset from one where I am unhappy about what I don't have to one where I am grateful for what I do have. I have four beautiful children, a wonderful wife, I own a house, have three square meals a day and people whom I can call my friends. So, to be honest, it doesn't matter if people think I don't drive a fancy car or wear the most fashionable clothes. I know what I have in my life and I am grateful for it. And my wish is that you too can gain a better understanding of your emotional triggers and overcome them.

Let me tell you a story about poverty scars

Many of us have poverty scars. You get them from experiences of not having things when you were growing up. When I was a child my parents couldn't always afford to send me on school trips, and this is something I still remember to this day. When I got to secondary school, everyone had Adidas, Nike or Puma trainers – those were the kinds of brands you had to wear to be cool. Unfortunately for me, I had none of those. I recall one time in school there was a trend where everyone had to have trainers which light up. And I remember begging my mum for them. She'd be like, 'What, do you think money grows on trees? Or money grows on my head? I keep the lights on at the house, why do you want lights on your feet!' Kids can be mean as well. Instead of the light-up trainers, I would show up to school in trainers with the fake Nike tick or the four stripes – and kids would make fun of me for that.

And so when I got older and started making money at age 18, I started buying trainers, obsessively. I used to buy multiple pairs in different colours. This is what we call 'poverty scars'. I wasn't buying the trainers because I needed them; sometimes I didn't even want them. I was buying them for the inner child in me who was still in pain from all the children who used to tease him at school.

What we tend to do in response to poverty scars, instead of dealing with the pain and going to therapy, is to use retail therapy; we end up buying more and more stuff to try and make ourselves feel better. But it's never enough. The real financial consequence of this is that you don't have money to invest or build with because you've spent it all on 'stuff'.

It's really important to take time to actually understand why you're spending. Why do you want to buy item X so much? And when you start to think about it, maybe a childhood memory might come rushing back that you can finally do something about. Once you start to love yourself and appreciate yourself and who you are, you can put these moments behind you as a phase in your life. You don't need to hold on to it forever. That will help you going forward. Your value is not defined by the things you can buy, the holiday you go on or the clothes you wear; you are already special, you are already valuable and you have to love yourself the way you are. Once you have truly understood this concept the way you look at and use money will completely change.

9

The UK Credit System

Within the UK system, your relationship as a borrower is one-to-one with your lender or creditor. It's probably worth mentioning here that you should never attempt to take out credit in someone else's name or let someone else do so in your name. When the time comes for you to repay the money, the lender only cares about the credit file of the person who has borrowed, and they are solely responsible for making any repayments. But I digress! I can't talk to you about building wealth without talking about credit. It's by having good credit that most of us will be able to borrow enough money to buy our first property, take out a car loan or be approved for a credit card. The modern-day financial system runs on credit, so we must understand the ins and outs of the system in order that each of us can participate. If you agree, then let's jump straight in and talk about how credit works in the UK.

It's not just banks that are interested in your credit file

Your credit file is a collection of information about your borrowing and repayment behaviour. That overdraft you applied for when you started university? It's in your credit file. Your mortgage? In your credit file. That loan you took out for a massively overpriced Merc so that you could impress your Instagram followers? You got that right – it's in your credit file. Although many of us are happy to lend money to family and friends, whom we know and trust, it's a lot more difficult to lend to people we don't know. This is the position lenders find themselves in when everyday consumers want to borrow money from them. Borrowers need certain information about you so they can decide how risky it will be to lend to you or not. It's this information that is known as your credit file. Who's interested in your credit file? You might think it's just banks, but in reality it's many more than that. Employers, landlords, trustees, directors and anyone you might be involved with financially are interested in your past financial activity. This is why I sometimes like to call your credit file your 'financial CV'.

Credit reference agencies

The companies that collect data about your credit history are called credit reference agencies. There are three main credit reference agencies and they are the same in the UK as they are in the US. They are Experian, Equifax and TransUnion. If you have ever tried to check your credit rating before, it's very likely you were doing so at one of these three credit reference agencies. They display your credit rating as a score, to give you an indication of how good your credit is – but they all score you differently. The Experian score is out of 999 – this is the one which in my experience most people have heard of. Your Equifax score is out of 1,000, and your TransUnion score is out of 710 – don't ask me why. It's good to check your credit score with these agencies so that you can see how you're doing. You don't have to pay for this – you can use a free credit-checking service. Money Saving Expert's Credit Club will show you your Experian score, you can use a company called Clear Score to check your Equifax score, and a platform called Credit Karma to check your TransUnion score. There's also a great service called Check My File, which you can use to check all your credit scores in one place.

Do I need to take out credit?

'But Eman, do I need to take out credit?' is a question I get asked a lot, and my honest answer is 'No . . . but.' Rightly or wrongly, we live in a system where if you have never taken out credit in your name, you can be looked at less favourably by lenders than someone who has taken out credit and then paid it back. This puts people in a slightly ridiculous situation: in order to prove that you are responsible with money, you have to borrow money even if you might not need to. And then, of course, people who borrow money but don't pay it back, or pay it back late, are looked at least favourably of all. So what I say to people is that they should take out credit, but that it should be with the purpose of building their credit history responsibly.

So when should you take out credit? In my view, this can be done at the age of 18. Going to university or starting a new job is an appropriate time to take out a credit card. In both situations you may have to make unavoidable purchases such as travel, books and clothing, which can be put on the credit card and paid off in full. If used responsibly, this will give the young person using the credit card the opportunity to build their credit history early and well. And, for what it's worth, I much prefer credit cards to overdrafts, because at least with a credit card you don't have the illusion that you have extra money in your bank account which isn't actually yours. I know far too many people, myself included, whose debt journey started with a student overdraft.

How to improve your credit rating

It isn't always obvious what you can do to improve your credit rating, and if you've ever checked your credit score you may be baffled about what is causing it to go up and down. But as a general rule, if you want to improve your credit rating, lenders are looking for evidence that you are able to borrow money, use it responsibly and pay it back. To improve your credit rating, having a manageable amount of credit available to you and using small portions of it, while paying it back on time and in full, looks good in the eyes of lenders. The amount of credit you use versus the amount you have available is called your credit utilisation. As a general rule, if you can keep your utilisation at 30 per cent or less, this is looked on favourably by lenders. So if you have £10,000 of credit available to you across, say, a credit card (£5,000), an overdraft (£3,000) and a personal loan (£2,000), as long as you are using no more than £3,000 of credit across all three your utilisation will remain below 30 per cent. Other things which look good on your credit file are registering to vote, paying for bills in your name and keeping lines of credit open for a long time.

Things that can negatively affect your credit rating

If paying back money on time and in full can improve your credit rating, then, as you've guessed, paying back money late or not at all is a guaranteed way to negatively affect your credit rating. It basically shows lenders that you are not able to manage the money you've borrowed, making them less likely to want to lend you money in the future. One thing you absolutely want to avoid is called a 'default'. When you default on a loan, or any other kind of borrowing, you are saying to the lender that you are not able to pay off your debt. This can leave a mark on your credit file for up to six years and so is best avoided at all costs. Similar to a default is an IVA, or an 'individual voluntary arrangement'; this is where you agree with your creditors to pay off all or part of your debts. This can negatively impact your credit rating for the duration of the IVA, which can be up to five years. Having a county court judgement (a CCJ) is also something that can remain on your credit file for up to six years and is also best avoided. Other things that can negatively affect your credit score are having a credit utilisation of over 30 per cent, making new applications for credit, and having a small amount of credit available to you. If you have a bad credit rating it can become much harder to borrow money, and the money you do borrow might come with a higher interest rate than for someone with a better credit rating.

Rotating savings and credit associations

It's important for us to note that having bad credit isn't always the fault of the borrower. For ethnic-minority communities arriving in the UK from the 1940s and 1950s onwards, borrowing money used to be a lot more difficult. It's hard to participate in a financial system that you are just joining for the first time, and in some cases ethnic minorities faced outright discrimination from financial institutions. These groups had to come up with resourceful ways in which to borrow money without having to rely on the banking systems of the time.

Enter rotating savings and credit associations. This is the fancy name for what Caribbeans call 'Pardner' and African communities call 'Susu', 'Ajo' and many other names. Rotating savings schemes have been around for decades and are practised by communities all over the world. They involve a group of people all pooling their money into a central pot, for a set period of time, with each person in the group being given access to all of the money for a set period of time. One person with just £250 might struggle to save £1,000, but four people with £250 each can all take it in turns to access the full £1,000 from the group one after the other. There is a company that I've worked with that has taken the rotating savings concept and turned it into a company. It's called StepLadder, and through working with them I have helped dozens of people save over £100,000, using the money to do everything from getting on the property ladder to building an emergency fund and paying off their debts.

So while building a positive credit rating is extremely important, there are other ways to access finance if you are willing to work with others.

Let me tell you a story about credit

Let me introduce you to Julius. Julius is an 18-year-old student and he's just started at university. And so he goes to the bank and gets a student account – the type that comes with a free rail card and a student overdraft. But in addition to this, he also gets a student credit card. Julius figures he wants to be able to pay his own way through university, so he also gets a job on his university campus. So he starts saving money and every time he looks at his bank account he sees his salary and student loan and feels rich. After a few months he has £5,000 in his account, including his maintenance and the money from his job. He sees his friends driving nice cars, flashing the cash and buying out the bar, and he also notices the attention they get from women who don't even know he exists. By the summer, he uses £3,500 as a deposit and buys a second-hand BMW 1 series and tints the windows to keep up with his friends. His monthly payments are £400 a month and because of his age his insurance premiums are expensive, costing him £150 a month. Julius isn't a naturally reckless person, but unfortunately he has a minor car accident, doubling his premiums. He's now paying £300 a month. Before you know it, he's maxed out his overdraft and credit card and is using most of his money from his student job to maintain his car. Unfortunately he's now struggling to buy books for his studies, and he's having to rely on borrowing from friends.

He didn't budget for the actual cost of living at uni – rent, food, sports – and now paying for all of this is a struggle. Worst of all, he has this really lovely car outside that he just can't afford. It gets to the point where most of the money he's earning at his job is going towards paying his debt and maintaining his car. This starts to affect his credit score. Which goes down because, according to the credit reference agencies, he is so far into his overdraft and credit card that his credit utilisation is high. This means he's nearly at the maximum on all the credit that's available to him. So he decides to sell the BMW, work extra hours and take public transport until his debt is paid off.

The main lesson to take from this story is to live within your means, especially as a student. Julius also learns that just because he doesn't have a particular type of car, it doesn't make him any less of a man. His true friends, who liked him before he drove the car, also liked him after he sold it. Going forward, he promises to save up and make better financial decisions, not overstretch himself, or show off for the approval of others.

10

Borrowing 101

Welcome to the chapter on all things debt. Now I know you're probably thinking, 'I can skip this chapter because all Emmanuel is going to say is stuff like "debt is wrong" and "debt is the devil", or he is going to tell me that I should avoid debt at all costs.' This is simply not true. There is no problem with being in debt; it's more about what you are in debt for.

Donald Trump once said, with his whole chest, 'My father gave me a small loan of one million dollars to get started.' Coming from an African household on a council estate where my parents struggled to give me money for lunch but were always sending money back home to Nigeria (make it make sense), this isn't something I could instantly relate to. Trump was able to go on and become a multi-millionaire, which shows us that you can use money to make more money. For those of you who read this and say 'obviously', I ask, 'how come you're broke, in debt and have no assets?' That's what I thought – don't let me start @ing people! Keep reading and I'll help you change your mindset.

Carrying on from the Trump example, and before we get into the technical stuff (which is essential, so please take it in), I want to teach you a concept called 'Other People's Money'.

We can't all get a million-dollar loan, but if our credit is good enough we can take other people's money. No robbery required. For example, go to the bank, get a loan and then use it to make some more money while at the same time keeping and using your own money for other investment opportunities, as well as for paying your electricity bill.

For instance, you could have a business idea to resell trainers online, but don't have the cash to get started. If you have a good credit score, you can get a 0 per cent interest credit card on purchases for eighteen months. This means you don't pay any interest for eighteen months as long as you keep up with the minimum payments on the card, and can buy multiple pairs of trainers at a good price and sell them online for a profit. You pay the credit card company back their money and keep the profit.

This is a simple concept and an easy way to start making money. The problem is that you hear the words 'credit card' and think, 'Trip to Dubai, imagine the likes I am going to get', as if likes are a going to put food on the table. 'I'm just going to withdraw my likes from the ATM' – said nobody ever. Using other people's money to make *you* money is a game-changer and a must.

Every month, the **Money Charity**, a financial inclusion non-profit based in London, releases a monthly newsletter called *Money Statistics*. The newsletter contains a number of useful stats relating to personal finance and banking in the UK. This may not sound quite as exciting as the occasional emails you get from J3FF B3Z0S asking you to collect the £73,456,789 he has waiting for you in bitcoin. According to the charity, in September 2021 the average unsecured household debt in the UK was £7,119, and per adult it was £3,741. For secured debt it was £55,818 per household and £29,331 per adult. These are pretty high numbers, right?! However, it is worth explaining the difference between secured and unsecured debt.

Time for some quick facts. Whenever you borrow money from a lender, the debt can be classed as either secured or unsecured. A well-known example of secured debt is a mortgage; I'm guessing you probably know what this is, or at least have a vague idea. For those of you who don't, a mortgage is basically a loan you take out to buy a house.

I promise you the advice and wisdom I impart from here on will be a little more revelatory. A mortgage is 'secured' because the money you borrow is tied to the house you are purchasing. Fun fact: the word 'mortgage' comes from the Old French *mort gaige*, meaning 'dead pledge', meaning that the contract ends either when the money is paid off or when the property is repossessed due to non-payment. The risk to the lender is generally lower with a secured debt, so the amount of time you have in which to pay back the money tends to be longer – many months or years. Generally, the rate of interest can be quite low. Got it? Great! Well done. Now on to 'unsecured' debt.

Examples of unsecured debt include credit cards, personal loans and overdrafts. These types of debts are 'unsecured' because the money that is being lent to you is not tied to anything. The lender has only your credit history to go on (which we discussed in the previous chapter), and the promise you have made to them to pay the money back, making this type of lending more risky for the lender. This is why, in part, they can flagrantly bump you when it comes to the interest you pay. It's a violation so many people willingly accept. The amount of time you are given to pay back the money tends to be on the shorter end of the spectrum, and the interest rates are higher. While the lender has no guarantee that they will be getting their money back, you do run the risk of your credit rating being negatively impacted if you are not able to repay. This is called a default, and it is worth avoiding at all costs. More on that later.

For my next trick, let me give you an example of how unsecured debt can go wrong. This is a true story.

Meet Babatunde, also known as BT. Like many Nigerian men, BT likes to show off for the ladies, but the crazy thing is that his ego makes him show off even more around his male friends. So BT earns £40k per year working in IT. His friends also work in IT but earn a lot more as they are contractors with a typical day rate of £500.

One of BT's friends is getting married, and the guys decide to have the bachelor party weekender in Dubai (as you do). BT knows, given his current financial position, that he has no right going on the trip, but pride and FOMO stop him from using his brain. Instead he uses his credit card, with an interest rate of 28 per cent.

BT has terrible friends: they know they make more than him, and yet they still decide to split everything while hosting models on the yacht they have rented for the weekend. The stress causes BT to sweat and hate the alcohol as he sits and watches beautiful women absorb his money in the form of champagne, as if champagne were oxygen.

By the end of the weekend, BT has spent around £10,000 – 25 per cent of his gross salary – on 'enjoyment' that he didn't truly enjoy. BT can only afford to pay £350 per month, so he will have to part with £5,329.86 in interest. One weekend holiday just cost him £15,329.86! That's a 25 per cent deposit on a £60,000 property.

This is a perfect example of how your mindset keeps you broke, not the amount of money you are earning.

Next, we will discuss how to manage debt to ensure that you do not end up with any nasty surprises on your credit file or any missed payments.

Debt management

When it comes to debt management people like to feel sorry for themselves – 'Oh my goodness, I owe money, feel sorry for me, the debt collector's coming.' But a lot of the time, people forget to take into account that they've had fun getting into debt. Look at your wardrobe. Look at your stunning holiday photos on Instagram. Look at your belly – Deliveroo has taken your money. You're in debt for food that is in the toilet the next day, can you imagine?! My goodness.

Stop blaming other people and realise that you put yourself in the situation. Stop saying you want to do better, yet continue doing the same things as before. If you're going to change your situation, start by changing how you spend your money.

Do the right thing and deliver yourself from Deliveroo. Make some pasta. Have some rice. Consider what you need to change. Start to challenge yourself. See where you're spending money unnecessarily. And stop it. STOP IT. I'm not going to give you a magic formula, just stop it. Or forget it and find a way to enjoy being broke. Stop walking around with all your credit and debit cards. Stop having the mindset of 'If this one gets declined, I'll just use the next one' – No! What you should do is just take one card out. Limit yourself. Call it a spending card. Use Monzo or Starling. Put a small amount in, and that's what you live on. Don't give yourself access to all your cash. Even when you feel like you can trust yourself, believe me, you can't.

Nobody wants to have to default on a debt, rack up unnecessary interest payments or suffer the hassle of managing multiple different debts. Not only is it boring to sort out, but it can also literally ruin your life. This is why it's very, very important for me to mention that one of the easiest debt management techniques is to *only borrow what you can afford to repay and to repay what you owe on time and in full*. This might also mean that if you can make a purchase without having to rely on debt, then you might be better off not borrowing at all! There is absolutely nothing wrong with saving up for something and then paying for it with your hard-earned cash – check out Chapter 11 for more on this. Not everyone is Jay-Z.

You need to learn to accept that – you are not a rapper. Normal people need to save to spend on extravagances. You will likely appreciate the purchase more because you've spent time and effort setting money aside for it, and will have the peace of mind that once the product or service is in your hands, it's completely paid for.

When you take out a debt, it will be made up of these main components:

Balance – this is the amount you owe to the lender at any given point in time.

Term – this is how long the money is being lent to you for, or when you have been asked to pay it back by.

Interest – this is the amount you need to pay back to the lender in addition to the balance. If you take the amount of interest owed and express it as a percentage of the balance, this is the interest rate. For example, if you borrow £100 with a 10 per cent interest rate, you will have to pay back £110 in total. Quick maths.

Annual Percentage Rate (APR) – this is a percentage representing the total amount you have to pay back to the lender, including interest plus any additional charges over the course of a year. So if you borrow £100 at a 10 per cent interest rate, but are charged a 5 per cent fee to borrow the money, the APR is 15 per cent. This is the main metric which borrowers and lenders use to measure and compare the total cost of a debt.

What does all this mean for you? Well, it means that before you borrow any money you should ask yourself how much you need to borrow, how much you expect to pay back in interest and fees, and how long you have to pay the money back. It's a good idea to make a note of this either on paper or digitally. You'd be surprised how many people don't have a clear picture of how many debts they have and to whom they're in debt. I'm not just talking about Wally the Weedman from Streatham who allows you to tick an eighth every now and again (top tip: don't tick weed – in fact, don't do drugs at all – waste of money) but the companies you pay a percentage of your wage to every month without even realising.

My favourite type of borrowing is where I already have the cash available to pay off the debt, at least partly or in full. It seems a bit nuts, but it makes sense. I am using the debt as a way to spread out the cost of a large purchase and increase my cash flow. This is the type of borrowing that will help you to sleep at night. On the other end of the spectrum there's borrowing for items which are in no way affordable to the person taking out the debt, who has no clear plan on how it will be repaid. This is the type of borrowing which can leave you feeling like our boy Babatunde.

Debt problems

Debt is a serious problem, not just in the UK but worldwide. It shouldn't be something we feel comfortable being in. This means that if you've got debt problems, like bailiffs at the door, look at how you can raise some money to calm them down. Go into your wardrobe. What can you sell? Bags? Shoes? People think your Gucci shoes are fake anyway. Get rid of them. I don't always advocate for the hustle lifestyle, but when you're in debt and finishing work at 5 p.m., then sitting down to eat beans on toast while watching *EastEnders*, that's not OK. No, no, no – you need to be making some money. You need to be out there looking for ways to bring income into the house. You need to be on Deliveroo and Uber Eats. That's not to order, but to get work. Ordering is what got you into this mess in the first place. So eat your beans and get on your bike. You need to be out there delivering. Good at English? Start holding courses online for people overseas. Do not declare yourself bankrupt. If you've exhausted every option, then that's different, but before you go down that route try and work out a payment plan. I know you work hard, but can you really afford not to take ten hours out of your weekend to make some additional money? You can earn £20 per hour in some part-time jobs. Stop feeling sorry for yourself and take action.

If you do find your debt spiralling out of control, don't panic, and most importantly don't judge yourself. Don't judge other people either. Apart from those who deserve to be judged for their stupid behaviour. There is a lot of shame and guilt associated with debt; people often suffer in silence and blame themselves for the situation they have got themselves into. Nobody wants to be seen to be struggling, even though millions of us are. Here's how to fix it. The first thing you should do is stop all borrowing. Then write down how much all your debts are, their different interest rates and when they need to be paid back by. There are many ways to deal with debt problems, including two very well-known debt management techniques: the snowball and the avalanche methods, which we'll look at shortly.

Get help

If debt's keeping you up at night, speak to someone. There's no shame in it. Believe it or not, trying to keep up appearances for people you won't be speaking to in the next five years is madness and not worth ruining your life for. You know that guy you went to school with, the one you feel is watching your every move and hoping you fail, meaning you have to stunt on him? He's forgotten you exist. He's following you on Insta because he was hoping for a follow back to boost his numbers. He's not watching you. Stop watching him; watch yourself. If you are in debt and it's affecting your mental health, your ability to make ends meet or adequately manage your finances, then it could be worth speaking to a debt counselling service. There are many fantastic organisations in the UK which provide free, impartial debt advice and can help to liaise with your lenders on your behalf and agree repayment plans with them. Citizens Advice, National Debtline, Turn2Us, CAP and StepChange are just a few examples. They speak to hundreds of people in this position and would be more than happy to help you.

Snowball method

Take the list of all your debts and order them from the smallest balance owed to the largest. Every month, pay off as much as you can on the smallest balance, while making any minimum payments on the remaining debts. Do this until the smallest balance has been paid off, and then move on to the next-largest balance and repeat. By prioritising the debts with the smallest balance, you will gain momentum psychologically as you get rid of each debt one by one.

Avalanche method

Take the list of all your debts and order them from the lowest interest rate debt to the highest. Every month, pay off as much as you can on the cheapest debt, while making any minimum payments on the remaining debts. Do this until the cheapest debt has been paid off, and then move on to the next-highest interest rate and repeat. By prioritising the debts with the lowest interest rates you will pay back the least amount of interest overall, meaning more money in your pocket every month as you get rid of each one.

Debt consolidation

This is where you use a cheap debt to pay off one or more expensive debts in one go, and then pay off the cheaper debt for the remainder of the term. Borrowers can do this to reduce the cost of their other debts. As we will go on to discuss, you can do this with personal loans and certain types of credit card. If you are struggling with the cost of debt but have a good enough credit rating, consolidation could help you save a lot of money.

Now we've broken down the different ways to manage debt. Let's look at the most common types of personal debt in the UK and what they are best used for.

Overdrafts

It's easy to judge. I'm not going to get on to you too much about these. I understand why people have them – they're good for emergencies and unexpected payments. If we need cash super-fast, then they make sense. It goes back to what I said earlier about 'other people's money': if you see an opportunity which would allow you to make some good profit, then there's no issue with using an overdraft to fund it. Use it. Excellent. That's great. The problem with overdrafts is that they tend to have a very high interest rate – it's expensive money. If you regularly go into your overdraft, banks and mortgage companies will see you as being unable to manage your money. Credit cards are better for emergencies; if you pay them off at the end of the month, all good. With an overdraft, it's noted by the bank – they can see you are struggling. It can reduce the mortgage you might be given.

Certain people are out here living in their overdraft like it's the NFL and they're in the N-zone. They're IN there, not trying to go anywhere else. They live in their overdraft and are overwhelmed by it. They get paid, and that's the only day they're out of their overdraft. Then the bills come and they're back in it. They look at the money like it's theirs. Like 'I have £1,000 and a £1,000 overdraft, so I have £2,000' – no you don't. It's not yours. That money is not yours to spend. It's the bank's money – please understand that. You get thirty days' notice to pay it all back, and if you don't do so that's a default, which takes six years to come off. That's going to affect you getting a mortgage. That's going to stop you getting loans in the future. Overdrafts can be dangerous. So ask yourself, why are you in your overdraft? Have you got a big business deal pending, is this overdraft money going to help you make more? Or are you using it to buy Hannah and Mark from HR bottles of champagne? Think before you use it.

An overdraft is an agreement with a bank to be able to withdraw more money than you have in a bank account. For example, if you had £100 in a bank account and a £100 overdraft, you would be able to withdraw or spend up to £200 from that account. Going into your overdraft is called – you guessed it – being 'overdrawn'.

Overdrafts can be 'unarranged' or 'arranged'. An unarranged overdraft is an amount – normally quite small – that your bank account will let you be overdrawn by. This is to allow for things like direct debits coming out at unusual times, or purchases that just tip you below zero. An arranged overdraft is something you can apply to your bank for and is normally a much larger amount.

Banks charge interest on overdrafts: either a set daily amount for as long as you are overdrawn, or a percentage based on the amount you are overdrawn by each day. This amount is then removed from your bank account at the end of the month. Overdrafts can be interest-free too, which is something that is typically offered to students. Where interest is charged, unarranged overdrafts are usually more expensive than arranged ones.

Loans

Why do you want a loan? Any loans taken out for lifestyle or appearance-based reasons are not loans you should be getting, my friend. Keep your lips the size they are. Stay wearing Primark. It's all good. But if you're getting a loan to buy some video equipment that you're going to use to shoot content that could end up making you money, then that's a risk worth taking. I ain't got no problem with that. Do me a favour, though, and make sure it's a viable business idea, not some hare-brained, half-thought-out scheme that's just going to cost you money but will allow you a few months of saying you're a *insert cool-sounding job here* to try and impress people.

If you're taking out a loan just for enjoyment, and at the end of it you've got nothing to show for it, think again. Take a car loan, for example: you're taking out a £20k loan to buy a car. The car costs £20k. When you buy it it's worth £20k, five minutes later it's worth £17k. By the time you've paid off the loan the car is worth £6k. Don't forget that you have borrowed £20k, but you'll be paying back something like £22k. Mad. That is not good business. That's not how it's supposed to be, my friend. Car-related finance could be a whole chapter in itself, to be honest.

Here's a piece of trivia for you: loans are perhaps the oldest form of debt. In 'The Code of Hammurabi', an ancient Babylonian legal text dating back to 1755/1750 BC (the sort of thing intelligent guys like me read on a daily basis), it is written that 'the creditor may not take barley from the debtor's house without his consent'. Creditors (the people who are owed) and debtors (the people that owe) have been with us for at least 4,000 years, but while in civilisations past we used to trade wheat and rice with one another, today we now also loan money to each other. Financial loans can take many forms, which we will go into shortly, but the principle is very simple. An individual makes a loan to a borrower, and in exchange for receiving the money upfront the borrower returns the full amount loaned, plus interest. There are a few different types of loans; let's talk about them:

Personal loans are sums of money loaned from the lender to the borrower to be paid back within an agreed period of time. You can normally borrow as much as a few thousand pounds in personal loans, and generally speaking, the higher the amount of money borrowed, the lower the interest rate. Sometimes people use low-rate personal loans for consolidation purposes.

Personal loans can be secured, unsecured or have a guarantor. A secured loan is tied to another asset, which can be reclaimed by the lender and sold if you are unable to repay what you owe. An unsecured loan is given to the borrower simply based on their promise to pay the money back. This represents a greater risk to the lender, and you will typically have to have a good credit rating to be able to get one. A guarantor loan is given to the borrower on the basis that someone else will agree to pay back the loan if the borrower cannot. This is slightly less risky for the lender, so typically a lower credit score will suffice.

Payday loans are a type of short-term personal loan for a smaller amount of money. The cash is made available very quickly and lenders tend to promise very high acceptance rates. The downside of payday loans is that the interest rates can be astronomically high.

Remember Wonga? Many people thoughtlessly took out those loans with a short-term mindset and then felt surprised when they were in financial ruin the week after. It's easy to laugh at these people, but it's a common trap people fall into when times are hard or they want to impress their peers with material things. Previous exploitative practices by payday lenders have resulted in some borrowers having to pay back many multiples of the loan in interest. Since 2 January 2015 interest caps were brought in for payday loans, including the rule that no borrower should have to pay back more than twice the loan amount. The upside of payday loans are . . . there you go. Quickest list I've ever written. My advice? Avoid payday loans.

Car finance loans are used for the purchases of new or used vehicles. There are many ways to buy a vehicle, which we covered earlier in this chapter, but for those who do not want to lease a vehicle or buy it upfront, car loans provide an affordable way to spread out the cost. Let's be honest here – a lot of people are financing high-end cars just to look good. You're trying to drive a BMW when you have Nissan Micra money. Behave.

Credit cards are usually the start of most people's debt journey. Too many of us hear that a credit card is a good way to build up our credit score and get them before we can even know our way around our money. I know a guy who has a credit score of 999 and he has never had a credit card or a store card. It's not an essential thing. Learn to manage your own money. If you can't manage your little £100 saving targets, don't go and get something that provides you with access to £4,000 'free money' each month. These things can lead people into a LOT of debt – debt that can take years to pay off. Learn to be on point with your own money before even contemplating a credit card.

One way in which credit cards are good is when you can get a 0 per cent deal; you can then use that money to buy a holiday next year, today – if that makes sense. You'll get a good price for buying so far in advance, you can pay it off over twelve to eighteen months and it's costing you nothing extra. I personally only use credit cards if they're going to make me money or save me money. Me buying a holiday a year in advance has saved me money. Me buying some Louboutins on a credit card is not going to make me money.

Credit cards are the most common form of unsecured debt. They're also one of the newest forms of debt too; they're barely half a century old – the first credit card issued in the UK was by Barclaycard in 1966. Even if you don't personally use one, it's very likely you have an opinion on them. Maybe you might think they're 'dangerous' in the wrong hands, or perhaps you see them as an easy ticket to the latest Fendi bag or trip to Dubai.

Credit cards are unique in that they don't need to be 'paid back' within a set period of time, but they do need to be 'paid off'. It's best to think of them as an amount of credit that is made available to you which you have to regularly replenish. If you borrow money on a credit card, even if the interest rate is

0 per cent, you typically need to make a minimum payment to the lender before or by the end of the month to show that you can manage the debt.

If you owe more than the minimum by the end of the month, you can also choose to pay off your card in full. If you just pay back the minimum payments on your card you will be charged interest on the extra, and this can happen month after month. Do this for a few months and you might end up owing far more than you spent on your credit card in the first place. According to the Money Charity, it could take over two decades to pay off a credit card using just the minimum payments! This is why it's important to pay off your credit card in full every month if you can.

The thing to remember about credit cards, and of course all forms of debt, is that they are neither good nor bad, they are just a tool. Like a Scotch bonnet pepper, a credit card can be a welcome addition to a tasty dish or it can burn out your eyes and the roof of your mouth. It all comes down to how you use them. Another thing to note about credit cards is that there are many different types of credit card.

Purchase credit cards let you buy things without accruing interest for a set period of time. Purchase credit cards are best suited to buying expensive items (ones you actually need!), or for spreading the cost of purchases over the term of the agreement.

Balance transfer credit cards let you transfer money owed on one or more high-interest credit cards to a 0 per cent interest credit card. The 'interest-free' period on a balance transfer card can last for a period of months, making it a useful debt consolidation tool. The transfer potentially enables the user to combine lots of costly debts on to one card so that they can be paid off within a set period of time. You normally have to pay a small fee to transfer a debt to a balance transfer card.

Money transfer credit cards let you withdraw money at a 0 per cent interest rate, for a small fee, which can then be used as cash. This makes them best suited for paying off expensive loans or overdrafts. The 0 per cent period lasts for a set amount of time – normally a period of months – during which you can pay back the amount owed on the card.

Reward credit cards let you earn rewards points, air miles or cashback for making purchases. The user may earn a set amount of rewards per purchase, or may have to hit a spending milestone in order to qualify for a reward – there are different requirements for different cards. As with other credit cards, reward credit cards do normally have an interest rate attached, and so must be paid off in full every month to avoid charges.

Travel credit cards do not charge the user a commission for spending overseas, or when buying from overseas websites. They may also minimise fees when withdrawing cash in a different country. This makes them best suited to people who regularly go on holiday or make purchases in different currencies. They too normally come with an interest rate attached and should be paid off in full every month.

Credit builder credit cards are specialist credit cards designed to help people with low credit ratings or with little credit history. They normally have a low credit limit but a high interest rate and must be paid off regularly. They are best suited for people who are trying to rebuild their credit rating or haven't had much time to build their credit – for example if they've just turned 18.

What a lot of people might not know about credit cards is the purchase protection they offer to consumers. Under the Consumer Credit Act 1974, if you make a credit card purchase between £100 and £30,000, and the product or service either isn't provided as agreed or the vendor you made the purchase from goes bust, you are entitled to a full refund from your credit card provider so that you aren't left paying for an item you never received. It is because of this purchase protection that I recommend always putting an item that costs over £100 on to a credit card, and then paying off the card in full straight away. You never know what might happen!

I know you're thinking that I'm about go in on **Buy Now Pay Later** (BNPL). If you follow me on social, it can seem as though I don't rate this model or way of doing things. BUT. It can be OK. If you are good at managing your money, and you can get an interest-free way of buying things split into three payments, then why not. It makes sense. It's more than just using Klarna to buy clothes – maybe you need a new washing machine or mattress.

The issue is that people tend to spend more than they might otherwise have done. Because it's interest-free and the payment is split over three to four months, in people's minds it's easier to justify expenditure that they may, in another scenario, have decided wasn't worth it. Let's say you're earning £1,400 a month and you see an item that costs £600. Usually, you're not going to buy it. I hope you're not anyway. It's too much. But if you can split it into three payments of £200 it hurts less, so you buy it. Before you know it, you've racked up a few of these and your debt is mounting. My gosh. Basic maths eludes you. Basic foresight eludes you. It's going to add up and it's going to catch you.

Now take Instagram for example. It's free to use, because Instagram are making millions of pounds every day by selling us to advertisers. People are making money from you using the app. BNPL is the same thing. Companies pay a percentage of what you spend to the BNPL companies, because it's been proven to generate sales that may not otherwise have materialised, so they make more money. This is how it works.

Imagine you bang a little BNPL purchase with Boohoo. A quick re-up on the essentials. Understand that you are taking on debt to buy pants, socks and vests. You are robbing your future self to do 'drippy drippy' in basic underwear.

Technically, BNPL has existed for decades. As the name suggests, it is a type of borrowing that enables the consumer to obtain a product upfront and pay for it later – typically in monthly instalments. However, newer services like Klarna (est. 2005), Clearpay (est. 2014) and LayBuy (est. 2017) have given BNPL a huge resurgence in recent years. Previously BNPL was mostly associated with big purchases – white goods, household furniture and appliances. However, with the newer BNPL services, consumers can access everyday products from thousands of stores because they integrate with many online retailers. There is even a service called Flava (est. 2019) that allows people to eat now pay later. Yes – you can BNPL your KFC. The main BNPL platforms do not charge interest on the money borrowed, but most of them do charge late fees, so if you do not pay off your purchase in full and on time you could have to pay extra. Missed payments can also negatively impact your credit score.

A final word about BNPL is that some lenders do factor in BNPL usage when deciding to approve products like mortgages. From June 2022 Klarna has started to appear on credit scores, so this means that people who aren't responsible could be affecting their credit through a new avenue. Banks have been known to deny mortgage applications if they see BNPL usage which they think will make the borrower less likely to be able to pay back the mortgage.

When used responsibly, BNPL can be a great way to spread out the cost of a large purchase at a 0 per cent interest rate without the hassle of having to apply for a credit card or loan, but it is best used for purchases you would have made anyway, and not as a way to obtain items that were previously unaffordable.

Let me tell you a story about credit cards . . . and overdrafts

Before I start this story I just want people to know that when it comes to the difference between credit cards and overdrafts, it's all about perception. When you have an overdraft, because it's all money that you can access from the same bank account, it can feel like it's your money. However, a credit card gives you money which you have to pay off every month. It's because of this distinction that I prefer credit cards to overdrafts. I think it's crazy what happens with student overdrafts.

I used to have a student overdraft when I went to university, and in my first year it was £1,000, but then they increased it every year. So in my second year it was £1,500 and in my third year £2,000. It was interest-free during this time, but when I left uni it became a graduate account. This meant that it stopped being interest-free after a year. I spent the whole of university in my student overdraft and even when I got my first job I remained in the red, and so I started paying interest. But I was generally very good at paying off my credit card.

My overdraft use became such a problem that one day my bank sent a letter to my mum's house saying they would default me. This meant that I had maxed out my overdraft and was no longer able to afford the interest payments on top. Because of this default they reduced the credit limit on my credit card too, which sent me into a massive debt spiral. Looking back, I was very complacent when it came to my overdraft. I should have not been comfortable being in debt, but I am sure we can all relate to feeling that overdraft money is actually our money. I always say to people that the main purpose of using debt is to make you more money in the long run or in a genuine emergency. Best of all is if you can live within your own means and save up emergency funds. The banks are not giving you this money out of the goodness of their hears; debt is a multi-million-pound industry. So you've got to use it on your terms.

Conclusion

I hope you have enjoyed this chapter on borrowing. We have covered what borrowing and debt are, and how to borrow responsibly. It is important to note that debt is neither good nor bad if it is treated as a tool. We have discussed the importance of only borrowing what you can afford to repay (even if this means not borrowing at all!) and the different components of what makes up a debt. We have also discussed how to manage and stay in control of debt, and what to do if it starts to spiral out of control. Lastly, we discussed all main forms of debt in the UK and their uses. I hope this chapter helps to destigmatise the use of debt in your eyes and instead think about your relationship with debt and how it should fit into your financial arsenal, if at all.

11

Saving

Saving money is one of the most important financial habits you will ever develop. But I find that a lot of people don't understand what their options are. In this chapter I am going to explain to you the core principles behind saving. Why is it important to have money saved? Why not just spend it all? How do you use your savings wisely, and for what purpose? We will also talk about the difference between saving for the short term (emergency funds) and saving for retirement via a pension. Mastering saving as a habit will enable you to build wealth because having cash gives you options. If you have cash set aside, this is money that you can use to put down a deposit for a house, take advantage of investment opportunities, or see yourself through a difficult period if you lose your job or your car breaks down.

Before we dive into the nitty-gritty of savings, let me tell you about the Financial Services Compensation Scheme (FSCS) real quick. Whenever you deposit money in a bank, the bank has to protect the money just in case it goes bust. This is called FSCS protection and it'll cover up to £85,000 of your money per bank that you hold it in. It's very important that if you plan on saving large amounts of money, the account you hold it in is covered by this scheme. If you're ever unsure, you can always do an internet search. Now, let's talk about savings!

Protect your finances with an emergency fund

If you were to lose your job today, how long could you live your current lifestyle before all your money ran out? For quite a few of us, the honest answer would have to be 'no time at all'. Research has shown that 15 per cent of people in the UK have no money in savings, which means that they are one payday away from not being able to afford their mortgage, rent or bills. Given how unpredictable life can be and how easily a situation can change, it can be very risky to not have any money set aside for a rainy day. Not having emergency savings can also make you dependent on your employer, or whoever else you get your income from, which is not a great position to be in if you don't like your job, or if you want to be able to have options. This is why it's important to build up an emergency fund. An emergency fund is a portion of your savings that you don't touch but instead put in a savings account that's easy to access if the situation calls for it. There's no set amount an emergency fund needs to be – I usually recommend three to six months of living expenses – but any amount of money, be it £500 or £1,000, is a great place to start. Once your emergency is fully funded, anything that you save above that amount can be put away towards your goals or to take advantage of opportunities.

Cash is king

You may have heard the phrase 'cash is king' before. It's a saying that I didn't understand for a long time. 'What do you mean "cash is king?"' I used to ask myself. Aren't I supposed to be investing my money? The true answer is that, yes, while it is important to invest your money, it's also good to have a portion of your savings held in cash, because this lets you take advantage of opportunities. If all your money is invested all the time, this might affect your ability to buy into investments if they ever hit bargain prices. During the coronavirus crash in 2020, the value of many stocks dropped temporarily as the world grappled with the spread of SARS-CoV-2. It was at this point that I advised my clients to make certain purchases within the stock market with the cash they had saved. I had one client who made more money during the first coronavirus lockdown than he had done during any other period of investing in the stock market. So the next time you hear the phrase 'cash is king', make sure you take it seriously.

Saving towards your goals

We live in a world of instant gratification right now – times are very interesting. When I was younger I never had the fanciest clothes or the latest toys, but I feel that back then, at least there was an expectation that you'd have to save up if you really wanted to buy something. And in the days before social media the pressure to follow your friends was a lot less; it was just limited to whatever school you happened to be in and your immediate friendship group.

Today this has changed and the pressure is getting worse. You can follow every minute of someone else's life on social media if you really want to, and what with BNPL, online shopping and the rise of cashless and mobile payments, you can get pretty much whatever you want, whenever you want, without necessarily having the cash upfront. If I'm saving for something, I still approach it in the same way I did when I was at school. I take the price of an item, write down the date I'd like to be able to buy it, and then divide the total purchase price by the number of months between 'today' and that date. I am still a big believer in saving towards the things you really want, even if it means you have to wait. Relying on your savings to buy things is the best way to guarantee that you can afford them and makes you way less reliant on debt. And call me old-fashioned, but I think saving also makes you value the things you buy more because you've had to work for them. You may have a bunch of purchases on a credit card right now, but in future why not try saving towards your next holiday or for your next designer item.

'But I keep dipping into my savings'

Dipping into your savings is a common problem, and it's often related to the issue of instant gratification. Rather than wait until you can afford a particular item, you go into savings which you have set aside for something else and buy it straight away. In response to this I say, 'Why are you dipping into your dreams?' When it comes to money I speak a lot about knowing your 'why', and this could not be more important than on the topic of saving. To be honest, the reason why we dip into our savings is because we have not designated a purpose for the money we have set aside. If we knew that the money was for a rainy day, or for a deposit on a house, we would be way less likely to use it to buy a designer T-shirt or on car finance we can barely afford. If you want to kick the habit of dipping into your savings for good, you need to get in touch with the 'why' behind your saving the money in the first place. Nowadays this is easier to do than ever before, with app-based banks like Monzo, Starling and Revolut offering spending 'pots', 'spaces' and 'vaults' where you can put your money away so that it is separate from your main bank account. These apps will even let you upload a picture of what you're saving towards and give the spending pot a name if visualisation is your thing. Keeping your savings in a separate account to the one that you spend from is an effective way of removing the temptation to dip in. It can also ensure that you are making your savings work for you.

Different types of savings accounts

Did you know that when you save money with a bank, you are actually giving them permission to lend this money elsewhere? This is a main way in which banks make money. They take deposits from Customer A and pay them interest and then lend them to Customer B while charging interest. The reason why they pay customers interest on their savings is to incentivise them to deposit their money with them. This is why I always find it a bit painful when I speak to clients who have huge amounts of non-emergency savings sitting in a bank account while earning no interest. There are many different types of savings account, each with a slightly different purpose, but it's very important that you use them and earn interest on your hard-earned savings.

Easy access and regular savers

Easy-access accounts – the clue is in the name – are savings accounts which let you access your money as and when you need it. Because you can access your money easily, the amount of interest they pay is on average the lowest. Regular savings accounts require the person saving to put aside a set amount of money every month, in exchange for a slightly higher interest rate than a standard easy-access account. The standard savings period for a regular savings account is one year – for example, a regular savings account might require you to save £300 a month for twelve months, so eventually you will have £3,600 saved. At the end of the savings period you get a lump-sum interest payment, and this is calculated based on the cumulative amount of money you have saved each month. The way interest is paid on a regular savings account can be confusing: if you save £3,600 in a year at a 10 per cent interest rate, you aren't paid £360 in interest. The interest payment will be slightly less, because it's calculated based on the total amount you have in the account each month.

Notice and fixed-rate accounts

Notice accounts are savings accounts which require you to give 'notice' to your bank before you can withdraw your money. A typical notice period can be anywhere from thirty to ninety days, and because you have to wait a little bit before you receive your money, you can expect to earn a higher interest rate than in an account where your money is more easily accessible. There are also fixed-rate savings accounts. In these types of accounts, you lock your savings away for an even higher interest rate still. The lock-in period can be as long as one or even two years, and if you need to withdraw your money early you may have to pay a withdrawal penalty. Notice and fixed-rate accounts, then, are best for savings that you don't need to access right away, and less suitable for emergency savings or rainy-day funds.

Premium Bonds

You may have heard of Premium Bonds but might not understand what they are. Premium Bonds are a type of investment product created by National Savings and Investment (NS&I), a UK state-owned savings bank. The way they work is that when you buy Premium Bonds you're entered into a monthly draw with prizes of between £25 and £1 million tax-free. You need to be at least 16 years-old to buy Premium Bonds and you can buy between £25 and £50,000 worth. Each Premium Bond has a unique bond number, and it's the bond numbers that give you a chance to win the prize once the bond has been held for over a month. The advantage of Premium Bonds is that you can buy them for yourself or for your child, grandchild or great-grandchild, and any money you win is, as mentioned, free from tax. But because there is only a chance that you will win in the prize draw every month, Premium Bonds are not great for people who want guaranteed interest on their savings. The fact that you don't earn regular interest also makes the money you hold in Premium Bonds at risk of losing its value over time due to inflation. You can sell your Premium Bonds at any time without a penalty, and your money is safe as it's covered by the FSCS.

Cash ISAs

Many of us have heard of Cash ISAs but might think of them as regular savings accounts. This couldn't be further from the truth! A Cash ISA is a special type of savings account because any interest that you earn is sheltered from tax. Money that you earn in interest is usually classed as income – because the bank is paying you to save your money with them. At the moment you can earn up to £1,000 interest free from tax each tax year – every April to March – but then after that you start to get taxed as if it were income. With a Cash ISA you never pay tax, not a penny. But you can only put £20,000 into them each tax year. The idea is that you try to 'max out' your ISA every tax year, to the point where you are making huge gains in interest. I must warn you, though, that when you put money into an ISA, it uses up part of your £20,000 allowance until the next tax year. So if you max out your ISA, but then withdraw the full £20,000, you cannot add any more money to it until the following April!

Saving to buy a property – Help to Buy and Lifetime ISA

Saving to buy a property? Eman's got you. You may have heard of the Help to Buy ISA, which closed to new savers in

November 2019. The Help to Buy ISA was an account designed to boost the savings of people hoping to buy their first home. You could put £200 per month into one – except in the first month, when you could put in a total of £1,200 – and save a maximum of £12,000 in total. When you came to buy a house, the government would give you a bonus of 25 per cent on your savings, after you had purchased your property. So if you max out your Help to Buy ISA, that's a maximum bonus of £3,000 and a total saving of £15,000. However, you can only save into a Help to Buy ISA if you opened one before November 2019.

In April 2017, the Help to Buy ISA was succeeded by the Lifetime ISA. The Lifetime ISA is also for people who are saving for their first home, but it's a bit more flexible. You can save £4,000 per tax year into one, but it doesn't have to be every month; you can do it all in one go or save monthly. You need to be between 18 and 39 to open a Lifetime ISA and you can save into one until you're 50. You get a 25 per cent bonus each tax year on your savings, so if you max out your Lifetime ISA with £4,000, you'll get an extra £1,000 from the government. One of the pros of the Lifetime ISA compared to the Help to Buy ISA is how you can access your savings when you come to buy a house. With the Help to Buy ISA you have to wait until you've 'completed' on your property purchase – which means you've signed the contract and you're waiting to move in. Help to Buy ISA savings can't be used towards your deposit and are instead more suitable for paying Stamp Duty, a type of tax you have to pay within fourteen days when you buy a UK property. But with the Lifetime ISA you get your full savings and your bonus before you complete, which means you can use it towards your deposit. Putting down a deposit for a home is normally the hardest part as it can often be a huge sum of money, so this is very useful for first-time buyers. The limitation of the Lifetime ISA is that you can't use it to buy a house worth more than £250,000 – or £450,000 in London. Also, if you withdraw your money for a reason other than buying your first home, you'll have to pay a 25 per cent withdrawal fee, and so you might get back less than what you put in. The only exception to this is that if you choose not to use your Lifetime ISA savings for a first home, you can use it towards your retirement – but you can only access the money for that purpose at age 60.

Let me tell you a story about saving

Let me tell you about Tracy. Tracy earns around £3,000 a month working in marketing. And because she works in marketing, she always follows the mantra, 'I am my brand.' She always feels she has to look the part – she understands branding, and therefore she makes sure to spend money on her appearance. Because of this, despite having a take-home pay of £3,000 a month, she never seems to have any money for savings. Her living costs are only £1,000 a month, so she could easily be saving £2,000 if she needed to, but she doesn't see the value in it.

One day, Tracy came across my page on social media and thought, 'You know what, I need to have a consultation with this guy.' She liked one of my videos and felt that maybe she could learn something. It turned out that one of her big goals was to move out of her mum and dad's house and buy her own place. During her consultation we figured out that to buy her dream home, she'd probably need a £30k deposit. When I asked her how much she had in savings, she said she had nothing. Then I asked her where she'd been spending all her money; it turned out that her wardrobe was her house deposit! She had designer bags – plural – that cost thousands. Shoes worth hundreds of pounds. Clothes that are beautiful, and extremely expensive. Then we started to talk about her holidays. It turned out she'd gone on five holidays in the last few years, at an average spend of £3,000 per holiday. So that's £15k just on holidays, for the mathematicians that are following the story. When we added up all her spending on luxuries, we found that she had easily spent £35k.

I first spoke to Tracy in 2020 during lockdown. It was a time of reflection; she was forced to stop and think about herself, and what she wanted to achieve from life. Following our work together she now has an emergency fund, she's paying into a pension and she is saving towards a house deposit. Having emergency savings means that if she were to lose her job she'd have something to fall back on, and once she builds up her deposit she will be able to realise her dream of moving out of her parents' house. The big lesson is that sometimes we need to stop; we are always on the go, our alarm wakes us up, we work, come home, sleep and the cycle begins again. Take the time to invest in yourself and not someone else's brand. I am telling you this story to encourage you to do so. Don't give your money to these other brands that will turn you into a walking billboard and meanwhile your finances are stuck in the same place but with no ownership. Some of you will only buy a certain brand, as though your parents are the CEOs or your family has shares in the company. Build your own brand and invest in yourself so you can change your situation. I hope this helps somebody.

12

Pensions

Now we get on to a very specialised and tax-efficient way of saving – pensions. This is such an important topic that I have dedicated an entire chapter to it. If you've ever been confused by how pensions work, don't worry, I'm going to tell you everything you need to know.

What is a pension?

A pension is a tax-efficient way to save for your retirement. It's for anyone who is working, earning or plans to retire in the UK. If you're working and you're making money, it's about putting some of that money away. And like I said, it's a very tax-efficient way to do so. If you earn between £12,500 and £50,270 a year, you're a 20 per cent 'basic rate' taxpayer and you will get that 20 per cent refunded to you on your pension contributions. If you earn between £50,271 and £150,000 (£125,140 from April 2023), you're a 40 per cent 'higher rate' taxpayer, and you can do a simple tax return and claim the 40 per cent tax back on contributions. Lastly, if you earn over £150,000 a year (£125,140 from April 2023), then you can claim the 45 per cent rate of Income Tax you would have paid as an 'additional rate' taxpayer. Remember that these rates of tax are not paid on your whole salary, but on the parts of your salary that fall within each threshold!

It's also worth saying that I prefer a pension to the Lifetime ISA as a way to save for retirement due to the tax relief you receive. Additionally, you can access money from a personal pension much earlier than with the Lifetime ISA (from 55, as opposed to 60).

When should you start paying into a pension, and how much should you contribute?

What I hear from a lot of my clients is that their priority is saving for a mortgage and that they're trying to put all their money towards that. However, the earlier you start paying into a pension the better, because it gives compound interest enough time to work its magic. I always recommend that at least 10 per cent of gross salary goes into a pension, but that doesn't all have to come from you, because your employer is legally required to put in at least 3 per cent as well. So 10 per cent is a good place to start, and if your employer offers a contribution match then do consider that too. If a 10 per cent contribution is too much, then start small. It is perfectly fine to start with, say, £50 a month and then build. I have clients who have started off at £50 a month, and then six months later they increase that to £75, and then to £100 in another six months. Increasing your contributions over time is a good idea because you get into the habit of it and you're less likely to notice it.

Are there any limits or allowances?

The annual allowance for a pension is £40,000 a year. The current lifetime allowance for a pension is £1,073,100. If you can get there, big up yourself! Once you get to retirement age you can withdraw up to 25 per cent of the money as a tax-free lump sum, and you can buy an annuity using the rest. An annuity is basically an insurance product that pays you an income for life. You can do this from age 55. As an example, let's say you had a retirement pot of £100,000; you'd get £25,000 as a tax-free lump sum and then you'd pay £75,000 to an insurance company. They would in turn say that for your £75,000, they would pay you an income of £5,000 a year for the rest of your life. You can also do what's called 'drawdown', which is when you withdraw and use the money as you wish. The UK government brought in this option in 2015 under a regulation called 'Pension Freedoms'. If you choose to go down the drawdown route, any amount withdrawn over the 25 per cent lump sum will be taxed as income.

Wait – your workplace pension is different to the State Pension?

Yes. When you see National Insurance contributions come out of your monthly payslip, that money is used towards public services like the NHS, but it also goes towards your State Pension, formally known as the 'New State Pension'. You need to have thirty-five years' worth of contributions to qualify for the full State Pension, and a minimum of ten years to get anything at all. The State Pension age continues to go up. It's currently

66 years, and is scheduled to rise to 67 between 2026 and 2028. By the time people my age come to claim it, it could easily be as high as 70 years. The GOV.UK website has an online calculator you can use to work out what your State Pension age is likely to be. What you definitely don't want is to have to wait for your State Pension before you can retire, as this might force you to continue working even when you want to stop.

You can access a personal pension or a workplace pension (i.e. a personal pension set up for you on behalf of your work) from the age of 55. But you can expect the workplace pension age to go up over time as well. So, in summary, you can access your workplace pension a lot sooner than the State Pension, and you also have more flexibility in terms of where the money is invested too. If you work in an industry where you generally retire younger, there will be specific pensions which allow you to take your pension earlier. Footballers are a great example of this. Also, if you are of ill health and are medically diagnosed as having a short period to live, then you can take your pension early. Other than that, there's no way.

What happens if I die before I take my pension?

If you die before the age of 75, your pension goes to your family members or nominated beneficiaries tax-free. If you die after the age of 75, it goes to your nominated beneficiaries, but at their highest rate of tax. A lot of my clients open pension accounts for their grandchildren (yes, you can open a junior pension! See page 189) and contribute to those. This sets them up nicely. It can be a great way to reduce Inheritance Tax, as the money in your pension is deemed to be outside your estate.

What pension options are there for people who are self-employed?

Pensions are amazing for people who are self-employed. If you are self-employed, any money that your business puts into a pension on your behalf is classified as a business expense. I like to advise my business clients to speak to their accountant before their tax bill is due and work out how much it is. Let's say there's a business with a £10,000 tax bill: what the business could potentially do is put that £10,000 into a pension and they won't pay corporation tax on the money, which will save them 19 per cent or £1,900. This is something that I recommend you speak to your accountant about before you do your tax return at the end of the year. Given that when you work for yourself you forgo the option to receive employer contributions, and because of the tax advantages, a pension can be a wonderful, wonderful thing for the self-employed.

Let me tell you a story about pensions

I had this one client who had been saving his pension for a while, and had a decent amount stashed away. He had £300k in a self-invested personal pension – a SIPP. And for those who don't know, you can borrow up to 50 per cent against the value of a SIPP and use it to invest in commercial property. So he borrowed an additional £150k and used the borrowings plus the £300k to buy his office. What this meant was that his pension became the landlord of his business. Over time, the value of the office rose to £1 million. Normally, you'd have to pay Capital Gains Tax on investment growth, which in this case was £1 million, minus the £450k – a profit of £550k. However, because the property was owned by a pension, there was no Capital Gains Tax to pay. All the profit was within his pension and growing tax-free. These are the types of things that can be done within a pension if you have the funds and the right advice.

I had another client who had two pensions. One had £9,000 saved in it, the other £13,000. But he consolidated them and used the money to buy a parking space. He also took out a loan to build some offices on top of the parking space. By renting out the offices and the parking space, again, all the money could enter his pension tax-free, and the value of the offices and parking space grew substantially, to about £250k. This is an example of how you can multiply your pension savings just by making some small changes.

A lot of people think they can't touch their pension savings until retirement, but what I want them to understand is that it doesn't mean they can't get value from that money. So start putting money into a pension as early as possible and build it up over time. Once you have a big enough lump sum, see a financial adviser who will help you look at other ways to grow and benefit from your pension savings.

13

Investing

Now we get on to what I am sure is the 'main event' for many of the people reading this book – investing! How to take your wealth and multiply it many times over. The funny thing about investing is that it can seem very exciting. I am sure many of us have images of *The Wolf of Wall Street* in our heads right now – people in suits yelling on the phone to their clients telling them to 'Sell! Sell! Sell!' Investing can be like that, but if I am going to be honest with you much of the investing I advise my clients to do is long-term and quite measured. We aren't trying to make a quick one or two pounds here or there, we're trying to build wealth for the long term. Building long-term wealth is not so much about reacting to the noise and doing what everyone else seems to be doing; it is about creating systems and automating the wealth-building process, focusing on increasing your income in order to be able to continue investing. In this chapter we will cover how you can get started investing today, with relatively small sums of money. We will also talk about the different types of assets you can invest in, and the strategies associated with each. We will even talk about crypto-currency, and why it has had so much press in recent years.

I hope you're as excited to read on as I was writing this chapter – so let's get into it.

Making a million is not the same as keeping a million

US financial expert David Ramsey did a 2022 study of millionaires, and the results were quite surprising. Among the 10,000 millionaires he surveyed, he found that 80 per cent of them invested in their company's 401k – the US equivalent of a workplace pension. Regular, consistent investing was the key to the investment success of 75 per cent of the millionaires, and only 31 per cent averaged an annual salary of $100,000 a year over the course of their career. One-third never actually made it to six figures in any single year they worked in their career. The reasons for this are simple – making a million is not the same as keeping a million. You can have an income of £1 million, but if your expenses are £1 million, then at the end of the day you will be left with nothing. Growing your wealth comes from the ability to keep your expenses consistently lower than your income over long periods of time, and then using the leftover money to invest. What many of us have been conditioned to do with this additional income is to use it to buy things. Shoes, cars, jewellery, furniture – and this is absolutely fine if that is what you want to do. But if you want to grow your wealth, then you need to 'buy' things that go up in value over time – assets – and minimise buying things which lose their value – liabilities. Once you have built up your assets to a certain level, you can then use them to create an income. For example, if you have enough money invested in stocks, you can live off the dividend income, or if you have money invested in property, you can live off the rental income. Once the amount of income generated from your investments is sufficient to support your lifestyle, this is what we call financial independence. It should be your goal!

The stock market

What do Amazon, Barclays, Alphabet (the parent company of Google) and Tesco all have in common? They are all publicly traded companies. This is just a fancy way of saying that they are companies which you and I – what we call retail investors – can invest in and become part owners of. Some companies are privately owned as well. Mars Inc., the company that owns Whiskas, Dolmio and, you guessed it, Mars chocolate, is still run privately by the Mars family to this day. But sometimes, when private companies reach a certain point, they sell off parts of their company to the public to raise money. When you invest in a company, that is money you have given them that they don't have to pay back. In exchange you become a part owner of the company, and if the company is profitable and increases in value, your share in the company also increases by that same amount. Investing in the stock market can seem like a scary concept, but thanks to technology there are so many ways you can invest in stocks. You used to have to rely on people like me to be able to buy the shares of companies, or even sometimes buy the shares directly from the companies themselves. However, nowadays there are many apps and online platforms which will let you invest your money from as little as £1.

Signing up to an investing platform

To invest in the stock market, there are three steps. You first have to sign up to an investment platform. Investment platforms are sometimes called 'online brokers' but it's essentially the same thing. Signing up to an investment platform can be done from the comfort of your own home, and you have to provide information similar to that required when you open a bank account online. There are some investment platforms that have websites, such as Vanguard or Hargreaves Lansdown; there are some which are app-only, like Trading212 and Freetrade; and then there are some which give you access to both. Once you have signed up with an investment platform, you need to open an account in which you will be doing your investing. Just like there are different types of accounts when you open a bank account – current account, savings account and so on – there are different types of accounts within investing platforms. There are three main types you can expect to see when you sign up to an investing platform: a general investment account or GIA, a Stocks and Shares ISA, and a pension account.

Opening an investment account

A GIA is like your standard investment account: you can invest as much as you like within it, but any growth you make on your investments or any money you receive as dividend income above a certain amount each tax year will be taxed. You are taxed on any growth above £12,300 per tax year; you are also taxed on any dividend income you earn above

£2,000 each tax year. If you want to shelter your investments from tax you can invest in a Stocks and Shares ISA, which works similarly to a GIA, but none of the gains or dividend income you make will be taxed. However, you can only invest up to £20,000 per tax year in a Stocks and Shares ISA, and you can only open and contribute to one per tax year. Your Stocks and Shares ISA allowance is also shared with any money that you put into a Cash ISA or a Lifetime ISA, which I have spoken to you about in Chapter 11. Lastly, many investment platforms offer pension accounts, either managed personal pensions, with set investment plans, or self-invested personal pensions (SIPPs), where you can manage your pensions yourself. Pension accounts are explained in full in Chapter 12.

Selecting your investments

Once you have signed up to an investment platform and opened an investing account, you can then select your investments. Obviously, you can invest in company shares if you want to, but be on the lookout for dealing fees, as some platforms will charge you a fee when you buy and when you sell. The platforms that don't do this are called 'commission-free' and will let you buy and sell shares without fees. The price of shares changes throughout the day when the market is open – 8 a.m. until 4.30 p.m. in the UK – and when you buy shares they normally appear in your account straight away, at the price they are advertised within your investing platform.

I often have people asking me, 'Which shares should I buy?' Meanwhile they have an iPhone, go to Starbucks every day, and always wear the latest Nike trainers. Nobody can predict how the stock market will behave in the short term, but these are all companies whose products many of us have spent hundreds of pounds on – and we have never even thought to buy one share in them. You can play the buy low, sell high game with stocks, but ultimately it is the companies that are used by people all over the world consistently, day in day out, which stand the test of time in the stock market. Of course, not all companies do well, and some go out of business completely – look at what happened to Blockbuster Video when Netflix came on the scene – and so I always advise my clients to diversify their stock market investments so that they don't have all their eggs in one basket. You can do this either by buying and holding multiple stocks at the same time – a portfolio – or by investing in funds.

Funds and ETFs

I really like investing in funds because it's a way of diversifying your portfolio at a low cost, and without having to do a huge amount of work. When you invest in funds, rather than buying the shares of a company directly, you can give your money to a company or to a fund manager who will buy the shares on your behalf. Sometimes a fund can contain a handful of companies, although sometimes it can contain hundreds or even thousands. What sets different funds apart is whether they are trying to 'beat the market' or just track it. If you invest in what's called an 'active' or 'managed' fund, then you are giving your money to a fund manager who has looked at the stock market and thinks that they have identified either a sector or a particular group of companies that is doing better than everyone else. You can get tech funds, funds based on particular countries, and so forth. The thing with managed funds is that they can be expensive to invest in, and fund managers don't always get things right. Neil Woodford is a high-profile example of a former UK fund manager who lost his customers money, taking some weeks to withdraw their money from his fund. For beginner investors, I like 'passive' or 'tracker' funds. These types of funds are not trying to beat the market; all they are trying to do is replicate it. So if the market goes up 7 per cent, the fund goes up by the same amount. You can buy tracker funds based on the UK stock market – the FTSE – or the US stock market – the S&P500 – and much, much more. I like tracker funds because they enable investors to invest a small amount of money each month and grow their wealth over time, without worrying about when to buy and sell.

Let's not forget Exchange Traded Funds or ETFs. ETFs are funds that you can buy and sell instantly like a stock, but the underlying asset in an ETF isn't just one company – it's a selection of companies, much like in a fund. ETFs were developed in the 1970s to help people buy and sell funds a bit more easily, as buying traditional funds can take a few days to clear because the investor is not buying the shares in the fund directly.

Ethical and halal investing

A growing number of my clients are becoming interested in investing in line with their values. I am very pleased to see the number of options that are now available for people who might not want to invest in mainstream stocks and funds. 'Why might someone not want to invest in a mainstream fund?' I hear you ask. Well, you might have a Muslim investor who would like to avoid putting money into alcohol, or a climate change activist who does not want to invest in fossil fuel companies. There are investment platforms that specialise in both of these. Wahed Invest is a halal investment platform, for example, and Triodos Bank is a Dutch bank known for its ethical investment options. The pros of investing in line with your values are clear: you get to make money in a way that is good for people and the planet. However, one of the cons is that some of the companies that people might want to avoid do make a lot of money, and therefore might perform well as stocks or in funds – tobacco companies are a great example of this. But if you were never planning to invest in a particular type of company, you probably wouldn't see this as a 'con' anyway.

Cryptocurrency and NFTs

When it comes to cryptocurrency, I might surprise a few people with what I have to say. I think cryptocurrency is the future, but not necessarily as a currency, more as a technology – blockchain technology specifically. On the currency side, it's clear that we are moving towards a future where we will see more cashless payments and more borderless transactions. I think about countries like Nigeria, where it isn't always straightforward to send money; cryptocurrency has completely changed that. Now you can send bitcoin back and forth seamlessly between two crypto wallets. I also think cryptocurrency has a part to play in creating currency stability. Look again at Nigeria, a country in which the currency has been hyperinflated: it was around 250 naira to £1 about twenty-five years ago compared to as much as 500 naira to £1 in recent years. Cryptocurrency could in the future provide a global monetary and payments system which is more reliable and trustworthy. But – I also think cryptocurrency is a very high-risk investment, and that you should only invest what you can afford to lose. For every success story you hear about people making thousands of pounds in bitcoin, Ethereum and so on, there are people on the other side of the cryptocurrency market losing money. So if you struggle with technology at the best of times, you might want to reflect on whether you actually understand cryptocurrency well. Don't get me wrong, though: there's money to be made, particularly if you educate yourself and speak to people who do understand it.

Let me tell you a story about investing

Let me tell you about Eric! Eric has some money saved in a savings account. He's a cautious man, and so doesn't like the idea of investing. He had a family member who had a bad experience and lost a lot of money in the stock market, so he has decided it's not for him. All that being said, Eric came in to meet me for a financial review and I asked him whether he would invest in the financial markets. He said, 'Me? No I don't do that stuff.' What Eric needed to realise was that while there is no such thing as a completely risk-free investment, there is always a risk to not investing, because of inflation. Inflation is eating at your money every day. You might not be aware that the cost of everything is going up, but over time it is. By not investing we reduce the spending power of our money.

I explained to Eric that he has all his money in a savings account earning him 0.1 per cent interest, so if he had £10,000 in savings, he's getting £10 in interest over the course of a year, or 83p per month. But if he took even a quarter of that money and invested it in the stock market and made a 7 per cent return – which is the historic average – he'd make £175 on that £2,500. The lesson here is that you don't have to invest all your money, but you have to at least try to make some of it work for you.

What many people don't realise is that when Eric saves that £10,000 in the bank, the bank invests his money. They use his money and everyone else's savings and deposits and loan it to other people. They're making money off our money. The only person not making money in this scenario, by leaving his money in a savings account, is Eric. The bank took his money, they loaned it out, and then they gave him 0.1 per cent.

Eventually Eric got the picture and understood what needed to be done. Eric now invests, but he doesn't invest all of it. Some of his money is in passive funds that he doesn't have to think about, and some of it is in stocks that he picks and watches. The rest is in cash, and that's absolutely fine. The point here is that you work hard for your money, so make your money work for you. Investing is a great way to do this.

14

Property

In my experience, property is an asset class to which many of us have an emotional attachment. Most of us live in homes, and they are physical assets that you can reach out and touch. There are plenty of books that specifically deal with the subject of property, but in this chapter I am going to talk about the various ways in which you can get on the property ladder, some of the more popular investment strategies associated with property, and why you might want to consider them.

Buying a home to live in

If you want to buy a home to live in, you're going to need a mortgage. As we have seen, a mortgage is a loan that is provided to you in order to purchase a property. There are two main types of mortgage in the UK: 'repayment mortgages' and 'interest-only mortgages'. Most residential properties are bought using repayment mortgages, meaning that you pay back the interest and the capital (the amount that you have borrowed). However, buy to let properties are normally bought using an interest-only mortgage, meaning that over the course of the mortgage you only pay back the interest, but don't make any payments towards the actual amount that you borrow.

'Loan to value' (or LTV) is the ratio between the value of the property you're trying to buy and the value of the mortgage you take out to buy it. For example, if my house is worth £100,000 and the mortgage is £70,000, the loan to value is 70 per cent. My deposit of £30,000 would make up the remaining 30 per cent.

Are mortgage rules different for first-time buyers versus existing homeowners?

The rules don't differ per se, but there are benefits you can derive from being a first-time buyer. If you're a first-time buyer, sometimes products from different providers may include your legal fees or cashback. There may also be other benefits such as a free home valuation. Also, if you're a first-time buyer you can take advantage of 'Stamp Duty' allowance, which is a tax you have to pay when you buy a property in England or Northern Ireland; this is currently £300,000.

Deposit size is also a factor. First-time buyers have historically been able to take out mortgages with an LTV of 95 per cent (with a 5 per cent deposit). If you're buying a second property, much bigger deposits are typically required and so you might be looking at 75 per cent LTV mortgages and below.

What is the best way to go about finding a mortgage?

To be perfectly honest, if you have good credit and a permanent income, you can go straight to your bank, search the web or use a mortgage adviser. A mortgage adviser can help you to research the best deals and many of them will do this for free. Their payment comes in the form of a commission from the bank.

If you have credit issues, are self-employed, are on a low income or are buying a non-standard property (for example a building over a certain height), then you would be better off with a professional mortgage broker. A mortgage is a good debt, but it's still a liability. So while you do have a property that will hopefully increase in value over time, you still have to make your mortgage payments. If you aren't able to make the payments, the mortgage company can force you to sell your property to make sure that the debt is paid. Now, if we're talking about a property that you're renting out, not only is that a good debt but it's also an asset because you're using it to generate income.

Could you talk a bit about equity release?

There are two forms of equity release. One is where you sell your property, release the equity (i.e. the percentage of the property you have paid off via the mortgage), use it to buy something smaller and then whatever cash is left is yours. There are also products that allow you to remain in your property but take money out. Something I'm seeing a lot now is that people are doing this to give money to their grandchildren, who can in turn purchase a property. This type of equity release is classed as a debt on your estate.

Could you describe the different schemes set up to help first-time buyers on the housing ladder?

Well, there's the 'Shared Ownership' scheme. This is where you can buy a percentage of a property – it could be 25 per cent, 50 per cent – and you take out a mortgage on the part that you own and pay rent on the part that you don't.

As an illustration, if you bought 50 per cent of a property worth £100k you would only need a £50,000 mortgage, which as you can imagine is a lot easier to get than a £100,000 mortgage. You'd own 50 per cent of the property and you'd pay rent on the remaining 50 per cent.

I don't particularly like this scheme, because it makes you feel like you're a homeowner without giving you all the benefits of home ownership. As someone participating in this scheme you'll pay all the costs relating to the property, the service charge and so on – all of that will be on you. It will also be your responsibility to pay the mortgage and the rent, of course.

When you want to sell, it'll be up to the housing association which owns the other half of the property to decide the price. If you want to make any changes to the house, you'll have to get permission from the housing association.

Lastly, because they're only buying a proportion of the property, there is a tendency for buyers to not properly consider the actual price of the whole property. Let's say you manage to take out a mortgage on 25 per cent of an £800,000 property (£200,000). That's *still* an £800,000 property that you're buying. When you come to sell, how many people are realistically going to be able to afford that? The buyer would have to be able to qualify for the Shared Ownership scheme as well. These are all things to bear in mind.

Help to Buy

The next scheme is 'Help to Buy' that is only available until 2023. It allows you to put down a 5 per cent deposit on a property, and then borrow a percentage of the property price from the government. This is called an 'equity loan' and is 20 per cent if you're outside London or 40 per cent within London. You would then take out a mortgage on the remaining sum.

The government loan is interest-free for the first five years, and after that you begin to pay the interest but not the capital. At this point you have a choice – you can either remortgage and repay the government loan or you can sell the property, but you will have to pay back to the government the 20 per cent or 40 per cent in order to pay off the equity loan.

The benefit of Help to Buy is that because of the equity loan, the size of mortgage you have to take out is much less. If you were buying outside London you would only need a 75 per cent mortgage, and because of this you would get much better rates. Your interest rate will be a lot lower, as will your monthly payments. And, as I said, there's nothing to pay on the equity loan for five years.

The strategy I advise my clients to follow is to aim to sell or remortgage the property within the five years, or save enough to pay off the equity loan and remortgage. Another route you could take is to sell the property after five years; and by then, after you have repaid the equity loan to the government, hopefully house prices will have appreciated and you will have a bigger deposit to put into your next property.

Tell us about the Lifetime ISA!

The 'Lifetime ISA' (LISA) is a tax-free savings account that allows you to save up to £4,000 per tax year and the government will pay a 25 per cent bonus (£1,000) on your contributions. It's a great way to save as you get the bonus upfront – you can actually use that money for your deposit. With the predecessor to the LISA – the Help to Buy ISA – you only got a bonus once you had completed your purchase. So the bonus was more appropriate for furniture or moving costs.

The only negative with the LISA is that there are withdrawal charges if you wish to take your money out. So you need to be absolutely sure that you want to purchase a property when you start to save into a LISA. Despite this, if you're buying a house for the first time the advantages of saving into a Lifetime ISA are great.

Finally, how can The Eman Effect help people who are looking for a mortgage?

There are qualified mortgage advisers within my company and I work with specialist brokers as well. I am able to help anyone buy a house, whether they've got good or bad credit, a big deposit or a small deposit; I can also help with financial plans.

Financial plans are super-important, and I can help people put together a property plan years in advance, while looking at how much they will need to save and borrow.

Buying a property to sell on

One of the main ways you can make money from property investment is to buy low and sell high. Many homeowners who bought properties over the last twenty to thirty years would have made money on them due to house price appreciation. A 2019 study by Halifax found that UK house prices had increased by 207 per cent since the start of the twenty-first century alone. However, simply buying a house and hoping it goes up in price isn't the most reliable strategy because, as with all markets, while the value of property does go up over the long term, it can fall in the short term. Just ask anyone who bought a house in 2007 or 2008. A more commercially minded buy-low, sell-high strategy is called 'BRRR', which stands for 'Buy, Refurbish, Refinance, Rent'. This is where you take out a loan to buy a low-valued property, increase the value of the property by refurbishing, repairing or extending it, and then get a mortgage on the newly valued property. Because the amount of money the lender is willing to lend on the property is now much more than what you initially paid to buy it, you can pull your money out of the mortgage and use it to pay back the loan and/or buy another property. Refurbishing a house can be a very involved process, but if home renovations are your thing, this could be the strategy for you.

Renting out a property

If you plan on holding on to your property after you've bought it you can either rent it out to a household as a Buy to Let property (BtL), or to multiple households as a 'House in Multiple Occupation' (HMO). Buy to Let is where you purchase a property and then rent it out to tenants. A HMO follows a similar principle, but is a property which is rented out to multiple households, or is converted so that it can house multiple households. In either case, as a landlord you will have a legal obligation to make sure that your properties pass standard gas and electricity safety requirements, that any deposit money paid to you by your tenants is placed into a tenancy deposit scheme, and because you are the owner of the property, you will also bear responsibility for the maintenance and repair of the fixtures and fittings. For a residential mortgage you would normally have to pay a deposit worth 10 per cent of the value of the property. If you plan to rent out a property either as a BtL or HMO you can expect to pay a much higher deposit, of at least 25 per cent. You will also need to demonstrate to your lender that the amount of rental income you expect to receive can cover the costs of paying off the mortgage, plus any expenses associated with the property. You can either choose to manage the property yourself as the landlord or you can hire a letting agent who will manage the process of finding and renting to tenants on your behalf, in exchange for a portion of the rental income. Many people don't realise that you can also list your property on an online hosting service like Airbnb and get management help from local hosts.

Rent to Rent

Another strategy is 'Rent to Rent', a property investment strategy that has brought a lot of success to sisters and business partners Stephanie and Nicky Taylor, the authors of *Rent 2 Rent Success*. On their website rent2rentsuccess.com they describe the Rent to Rent model in just a few steps. You rent a property, usually for three to five years, paying the owner a guaranteed rent for this period of time. Typically you would also assume responsibility for any bills. A landlord may be happy to allow you to sublet their property to someone else, if it means that they are guaranteed a steady amount of rent for a period of years and are fully aware of what is taking place. But it would be up to you as the 'middleman' to make sure that you are able to rent the property to tenants for a higher amount of rent than you are paying the owner. If you are able to do this, of course, then you make a profit.

Let me tell you a story about property

Meet twin brothers Ty and Kenny. Ty is the sensible one. Of the two he's always been the more risk-averse, building for the future and thinking about tomorrow. Kenny, on the other hand – Kenny has always wanted to live for today. He's always been the one to get more attention from women, even though they're identical twins. As they get older, Kenny goes out a lot, having fun, mingling with the ladies. Meanwhile, Ty is saving. They both live at home and they share a room. Ty gets to a point where he no longer wants to share a room. One day he says, 'I gotta get my own space and get out of this room!'

Kenny doesn't care about the room. He's always taking girls to nice hotels and restaurants – he basically comes home to sleep.

Ty works and saves, but Kenny works and spends. They're on similar salaries, but live different lives. Eventually, Ty manages to save enough money to secure a deposit and get on the property ladder. After about a year, Ty decides to rent out his out his two-bedroom house and move back into his mum's with his brother. Kenny doesn't understand this, saying, 'You wanted to get out? You got out, bought something and now you're back again?'

As more time passes, Ty and Kenny's mum would like them to buy her house, which she has been renting all this time using Right to Buy. Right to Buy is a scheme in England and Northern Ireland which enables council tenants to buy their homes outright at a discount, as long as they have been a public-sector tenant for three years. Kenny has been so reckless with his finances that his credit score is a mess and he can't even scrimp together enough money to save anything. So Ty ends up buying the house without his mum needing to use the Right to Buy Scheme. Instead he uses his savings and additional rental income from his first property. So after a few short years Ty is now the owner of two homes, Kenny is the owner of none. Kenny is now also paying rent to his brother, to live in the same bedroom they grew up in.

Ty doesn't stop there. He gets an extension on the house, pulls money out of his mortgage and uses it to buy a third property, a beautiful three-bedroom semi-detached house in the suburbs. This is where he ends up settling.

For me the moral of this story is that when you're young, look to build wealth. It's nice having watches and jewellery and so on. It'll get you attention from the guys or the ladies, but it'll be short-lived. It is assets and ownership that will give you freedom. You might not always be able to buy a property at the same time as everyone else, but building wealth should be front and centre: once you have assets that pay you a regular income, the world is your oyster.

15

Protecting your Assets

When it comes to protecting your assets, always remember that your most important asset is yourself. I don't say this as a soundbite, or just to throw the saying around. One of the most important forms of protection you can get for yourself is life insurance, and it is an accessible way for people to leave something to their loved ones when they die, even if they may not have a lot of money in the bank. A second form of protection I often speak about are trusts, which can be used to hold assets for your beneficiaries on your behalf. I have a lot of experience with both of these financial tools, and I know they aren't widely spoken of or very well understood; so in this chapter I am going to teach you about them and how you can use them to your advantage.

What is life insurance?

Life insurance is a type of cover that you can take out to protect your loved ones, yourself or something valuable to you.

There are three main types. There is standard life insurance, which will pay out to your dependants in the event of your death. Critical illness insurance pays out to you if you have a serious illness such as cancer, a stroke or heart attack. Lastly there is income protection insurance, which will pay out if you're sick and unable to work. The three types of life insurance I've just mentioned are also listed from least expensive to most expensive. Life insurance is the cheapest, because people are now living longer. Critical illness is the next most expensive, because more and more people are getting critical illnesses due to increased life expectancy. And income protection insurance is the most expensive because it requires you to be sick and unable to work before it pays out.

What level of cover is appropriate for a person looking to take out life insurance?

With life insurance, it depends whether you have an actual 'asset' you're trying to cover. For example, people normally tend to think about life insurance when they're getting a mortgage, and may get life insurance to cover the term of the mortgage. I always encourage people to think carefully about their dependants and the people they're likely to leave behind. Let's say you've taken out life insurance to cover just your mortgage payments. In the unfortunate event of your death, yes, your mortgage might be paid off, but how will your dependants continue to live if you're the main breadwinner? This is where we need to start thinking about the amount of income that your dependants are likely to need. Depending on your stage of life, a multiple of your annual income might be most appropriate – say ten, twenty or thirty times – but this will also depend on your budget. Normally, I would recommend a minimum of ten times the required actual income.

What is a 'term policy'?

If you want to leave an income for your family over a fixed time period there's a product called 'Family Income Benefit'. For example, a family with young children could take out a policy that would pay out £10,000 a year until their youngest child reaches the age of 25. This amount could either pay out annually until all children had reached 25, or could be paid out in a lump sum.

So how do payouts work in practice?

I always recommend that my clients put their insurance 'into trust'. This avoids clients having to go for 'probate'. I'll explain. An insurance policy that is written into trust can be immediately paid out by the insurance company to your trustees, based upon the instructions you gave while you were alive. It's relatively quick. If the policy is not in trust, it will be paid into your estate and your executors will have to undergo a legal process to release the money, called probate. The executors of your estate will also have to be assigned – which can take a while – and while all this is going on nobody can get access to the money. Finally, if the money is in your estate and if it is over the £325,000 Inheritance Tax threshold, then you could lose 40 per cent of any money over this amount to tax.

What affects the price of life insurance? What makes it cheaper versus more expensive?

One of the main factors is your age. I'm always asked the question, 'Should I get life insurance young?' and my answer is 'Yes!' The younger you are, the more healthy you are and the less likely you are to fall ill, the cheaper the insurance. Also factored in is your health, so insurers will look at your weight, BMI, whether you're a smoker or not. Things like being overweight or being a smoker can increase your premiums. There are also things which can affect the cost of your life insurance outside of your health and age. Life insurance that covers you for a set period of time is called a 'term policy' and insurance that covers you until you die is called a 'whole of life policy'. Term policies are cheaper than whole of life policies because, obviously, they only have to cover you for a specific period of time. So I advise clients at an earlier life stage to consider taking out a term policy, and then to consider switching to a whole of life policy when they get a bit older.

Can you switch life insurance providers if you see a cheaper deal or if you're unhappy with the service?

Yes, you can, but it's not a 'switch' in the same way you'd switch a current account – you'd have to set up a brand-new policy and then cancel the old one. Again you have to consider your age. If you're older and you decide to take out a new policy, or if you've developed any health issues since taking out the first policy, then potentially the price could go up. My advice is not to cancel your current policy until you've completed the underwriting process with the new one. You must also make sure that the price that you've been quoted is the actual price you're going to pay at the end of the process. Life insurance is protected by the Financial Services Compensation Scheme (FSCS). If the provider goes bust you will be able to claim compensation for 90 per cent of the cover owed.

A word about trusts

I can't talk to you about protecting your assets without telling you a little bit about trusts. It's very likely that if you ever set up a trust, it will be with the help of a financial adviser, but it's still important for me to tell you about them and how they work. A trust is a legal instrument that you can use to protect and manage assets like land, property, investments and money. Because the trust is not a 'person' it is taxed differently than if an individual owned the assets. There are people required in the creation of a trust, however. You have the person who places assets into a trust, called a 'settlor'; the manager of a trust – a 'trustee'; and finally the individual who will benefit from the trust, a 'beneficiary'. So, for example, you might want to pass on assets to your children, but only allow them to take control of them once they reach adulthood. These assets can be placed into a trust during their childhood years and released to them once they turn 18.

Another use for a trust is the protection of life insurance policies. Let's say a couple are planning to buy a house. It's standard in a scenario like this for both parties to take out a life insurance policy to cover the cost of the mortgage if one of them passes away. Now, if they were to take out a joint life insurance policy and one of them were to pass away, it would pay just the one time, leaving the surviving party uninsured and with a potentially larger insurance bill if they chose to reinsure themselves again. So I always tell couples to take out two single life insurance policies and put them into trust with each other as the beneficiary. This can be more expensive than taking out a joint policy, but it does mean that if one member of the couple passes away, the payment can be made immediately to the surviving member, who will remain insured. This is why it's worth looking at single policies in addition to joint ones.

Let me tell you a story about life insurance

I had this client, whom we'll call Mr Fisher. Mr Fisher used to come in when I was a cashier at a bank, and we'd often have conversations. Over time we got to know each other, and then I was promoted from being a cashier to becoming a financial adviser. I'd kept in touch with Mr Fisher, and one day I said to him that he should consider getting life insurance. And he agreed! He said, 'I know you're a new financial adviser, you've always been good to me since you were a cashier and I trust you.' And so we sat down and got him a policy with £400k cover, enough to give him peace of mind for his wife and his two kids. The monthly payments weren't even that much – he was pleasantly surprised.

Then one day, about eighteen months later, Mrs Fisher came into the bank. I had no idea what she looked like as

I'd never met her before. But one of my colleagues said to me, 'Emmanuel, Mr Fisher's wife is here.' She had come in to tell me that, unfortunately, Mr Fisher had passed away. I remember feeling so, so sad. He was a good friend. Mrs Fisher expressed her thanks to me for asking her husband to take out a life insurance policy and putting it into trust. Because we had put it into trust, everything had been processed quickly and the payment was on its way to her.

Initially she had been worried about giving him a good burial, and looking after the kids, but that was now all taken care of. I was overcome with emotion. I was sad about the family's loss, but happy that at least I had been of some help. Now, whenever I sit down with a client, I always look at life insurance, critical illness and income protection, because financial protection like life insurance can seem useless until you need it. Unfortunately I've had other clients who had life insurance but cancelled it and then had a heart attack, by which point it made getting replacement cover even more difficult – or, if they'd passed away, too late. It's so important to value life insurance. Get yourself protected, particularly if you've got dependants.

16

Generational Wealth

What is generational wealth?

It seems like the concept of generational wealth comes up a lot. Whether it's on social media, in conversations with family or with friends, people are very interested in passing on their assets to the next generation. It's definitely an attractive idea, especially when you come from a family that has worked hard to give you a good life, and you feel that same sense of obligation to your children and to the young people in your life. But let me tell you as a financial adviser, generational wealth is one of the least understood areas of finance. You can spend your whole life earning money and building wealth, but if you don't put certain things in place it does not necessarily follow that the next generation is going to benefit. In 2015 the US-based Williams Group published a study; you may be familiar with its findings. They found that 70 per cent of well-off families lose their wealth by the second generation, and 90 per cent by the third generation. So in this chapter I am going to explain what generational wealth is, and how to make sure that all your hard work actually gets to benefit the next generation.

Why pass on wealth to the next generation?

As I have said, I came from nothing. My parents moved to the UK in search of a better life, and to give me opportunities that they did not have when they were growing up. I will be forever grateful to my parents for the sacrifices they made and the example they set, and it's because of everything they did for me that I developed the drive to become good with money. My own children have not even gone through 1 per cent of the hardship I did when I was growing up, and this is as it should be. As a people, as a generation, if we're not moving forward, we're moving backwards. I believe that we have an obligation to leave the world better than we found it and to give the next generation the best possible start in life so that they can do the same. We should all be thinking and dreaming bigger too. I fully believe that we rise to the level of challenge we set ourselves. If you are only thinking about yourself, then you will build a level of wealth that benefits only you. But I'm not just thinking about my children, I'm thinking about their children, and the generation after that. I want to make sure that the Asuquo name stands for something – and in order to do this I am going to have to achieve much more than I would do if I was just trying to meet my present-day expenses and responsibilities. While this chapter will mainly focus on how we can pass on wealth to our own children and grandchildren, bear in mind that politicians, teachers and role models – anyone in a position of responsibility – are also actively contributing to the wealth of the next generation. You may be thinking of generational wealth simply in terms of financial assets, but, as I am about to show you, it's a lot more than that.

Financial education comes first

You've picked up this book because you want to better yourself and gain control of your finances. I applaud anyone who is willing to invest in themselves and put their own education first, particularly when it comes to finances. Why? Because without a financial education, any money that you do make will leave your bank account and end up in the bank accounts of people with a greater financial know-how than you. I realise that you understand this all too well, or you would not have taken the time to read this book. But it's not enough for us to just educate ourselves; it's on us to make sure that the lessons we've learnt are passed on to the next generation. This means that you must be sure to pass on to your children and the young people in your life the principles you have learnt in this book – everything from how to make and spend money to how to save and invest it. It also means that we need to be willing to continue learning about our finances as time goes on. In my lifetime, I have gone from seeing people queuing up in bank branches to access banking services to doing all their banking on a mobile app. While some of the core principles of finances will remain the same, nobody knows how technology will change the way that we manage our money or transact. So it's up to us to get educated and stay educated, so that when we do pass on our wealth to the next generation they are able to keep it, multiply it, and pass it on to their own children.

Your network can be your legacy to your child

Here is something you can leave to your children that won't cost you or them any money at all – your network. Throughout your life you are making connections, building relationships and making friends who have added value to your life. Everyone from your friends at school and university to your colleagues at work and partners in business – all these people have something to offer. Through my own work as a financial adviser I know athletes, authors, people in government and senior leaders in the financial services industry. This means that when my children are older, if there is a particular industry that they would like to go into, there's a good chance that I will either know someone in that industry, or know someone that does. Equally, if any of the people in my network approach me to introduce their children to one of my connections, or need an introduction within the financial space specifically, I will be able to do so. You've probably heard the phrase, 'Your network is your net worth'. This is absolutely true; and one of the most valuable things you can pass on to the next generation, other than money, is the network of connections you have made over the course of your life. I'm telling you this because I don't want you to think that just because you don't have money or material wealth, you have nothing to give. If you don't come from a wealthy family, make sure a wealthy family comes from you.

The family business

Do you run a business, or have aspirations to do so one day? If so, then the business you've worked so hard to build today could be something that your children one day do work experience for, or maybe even take over from you and work in it themselves. The problem with the business owners I know is that too many of them don't teach the next generation that their first business is their family business. This is something that I am making sure to pass on to my kids. All the jobs I worked in up until this point were good jobs, but in someone else's company. I couldn't get my children a job in my place of work just because I worked there. This has all changed now that I run my own business. My children see all the work I am doing as a financial adviser, online and in the media, because I want them to know what's possible, and that they have the choice to join me in the business one day if they choose to. If you are running a business, or plan to do so, your children should have a good understanding of what the family business does, the finances, the different roles within it and the day-to-day operations. I have seen far too many wealthy children who know that they come from a well-off family but have no idea what their parents do. Never me! However, I do not suggest that you force your children to be part of the family business. Everyone has their own interests and unique skills and talents, after all. But if they are interested in getting involved, the option should be there, and it is only fair that if they contribute to the family business they are also beneficiaries of it.

Generational wealth only works with health

Money is just one of the things I plan to leave to my children. I will also be leaving them networks, education and perhaps the most important thing – memories. What we need to understand is that generational wealth only works with health. It's all well and good having millions of pounds in the bank, but if you aren't eating or feeling right you won't be in a position to share experiences and create precious memories with your loved ones. When you look back at your own childhood, what is it that stands out the most? Sure, you'll remember presents you may have been bought, and the safety and security that a financially stable home can bring. But I also remember family parties, Christmases together, and nights spent watching films and playing family games with my parents and my sisters. Don't forget why we are building all this wealth in the first place – it isn't just to amass money for money's sake, it's to give the next generation the best possible start in life and to leave them with experiences and memories that will last them a lifetime. So while this isn't a book about health and wellbeing, I will say that it's important you eat well, prioritise some time in your day, every day, to get exercise, and to make sure you look after your mental wellbeing too. We all want to be here for both a good time and a long time.

Leaving behind an inheritance

I will of course be leaving my children financial assets, as this is a core component of generational wealth. For this you need to understand how Inheritance Tax works. You see, all the assets you currently own form part of your estate. The value of your estate is how much you would get if you sold everything you owned today, less any debts that you owe. This includes things like investments, property and land, physical assets, collectibles and furnishings. In the UK, as we have noted, you can pass on assets up to the value of £325,000 tax-free; anything which comes above this threshold is taxed at 40 per cent – wow. There are also things which do not form part of your estate. Jointly owned property, land or bank accounts do not normally form part of your estate and are usually transferred to the remaining owner on your death. Life insurance policies and pension plans also do not normally form part of your estate, and instead go to the people you have nominated to receive them when you pass on.

The seven-year rule

By the way – if all this talk of death is making you feel a bit down, don't be. If you are able to leave something behind to others when you die, it's probably because you did something right while you were still living. You might be interested to know that a trend I am noticing is that people are not always waiting until they die to pass on their assets. There is a way to 'get round' the 40 per cent Inheritance Tax charge, and that is if you gift your assets to your beneficiaries before the last seven years of your life. Obviously, because no one knows when they are going to pass away, this incentivises people to give away their assets well in advance of their death. A great way to do this is with a pension. You can set up a junior pension for your young ones from the day they are born and pay money into it while receiving tax relief from the government – up to £3,600 per tax year. They can take control of the account from age 18 and then continue to pay into it until they are at retirement age. I see a lot of grandparents doing this for their grandchildren, and I think it is a great way to give your child a head start in life.

Writing a will

Something I won't be doing with my children is letting them know how much they stand to inherit, or guaranteeing anything to them in any way. I want them to still have the drive to achieve something in their lives, and not expect a windfall to automatically come to them when myself and my wife pass away. Whether you choose to do this will be a personal decision on your part. What I plan to do, though, is write a will. A will is the best way to signal your intentions about what you would like to happen to your assets when you die, in a way that makes things far easier and transparent for those left behind. I always say that the best time to write a will is when you have dependants or assets. You will need to update your will at other key life moments too, such as when you get married or – hopefully not – divorced. Too many times I have heard stories about someone's grandmother dying without a will, and then all the children and grandchildren fighting over her house and furnishings. Put all of that to bed by writing a will and letting people know what your intentions are while you are still alive. You might be wondering, 'Eman, I don't know the first thing about writing a will!', and I completely understand that. However, what a lot of people don't know is that there is a UK charity will-writing scheme called Will Aid: you can get a will drawn up by a legal professional, and instead of paying costly legal fees you can instead donate £100 to charity for a single will or £180 for a pair of wills. You can read about how the scheme works at the website willaid.org.uk.

Let me tell you a story about inheritance

Should you tell your kids about their inheritance? It's a big question and I think it all depends on your relationship with them. I once had a client whom we'll call Claire for confidentiality purposes. Claire wanted to buy a house, and so I asked her the usual questions: 'Have you got a deposit? Any savings? What's your income?' Claire had no deposit or savings and was on about £20k. Yet she was looking at houses worth £500k. When I asked Claire how she planned to get her deposit together, she proceeded to tell me about how her mum was ill and in hospital and, I quote, 'on her way out soon'. Now it's a rather morbid story, but this is the type of thing that can happen when parents tell their children they will be leaving them money but don't explain their wishes or what they would like them to do with it. A trend I am witnessing at that moment is that a lot more clients are planning on giving their money away to their children while they can still see it.

I had another client whose name was Joanna – name also changed. And Joanna was adamant that she wasn't going to pay Inheritance Tax. From her perspective she had her kids, she had her grandkids, and had great relationships with all of them – she wanted to help them out in the here and now. So in her later years she began to help her children and grandchildren to be financially stable. She did something called equity release, which is basically when you take money out of your mortgage and then give it to your children or grandchildren. For her this was great. She got to go to her grandchildren's weddings and helped them out with the cost. She helped them get on the property ladder. And they were able to appreciate their grandma while she was still alive. The lesson here is that you don't have to wait until you pass away to leave behind an inheritance, but at the same time you don't need to tell your children how much they're going to get. This is the lesson drawn from the examples of Joanna and Claire.

What you should do is have a conversation with your family about generational wealth and make sure they understand the importance of taking what they've been given and increasing it. Generational wealth is when you can ask yourself, 'What can I do to add to what I have already received?' These are the sorts of conversations we need to be having. What generational wealth isn't about is inheriting money and using it all up. That's not how it is – not when it's been given to you. Ultimately, if we are lucky enough to inherit, it's our job to ensure that there's money to be passed on to future generations. This is how we can build more and more wealth as the generations go on.

17

Philanthropy

Once you've managed to get your own money right, and you're able to look after those closest to you like your family and friends, the next step in your journey might be to turn to issues in your community, or perhaps even global issues. There's a reason why many of the world's richest set up charitable foundations and give billions away to philanthropic causes. The wealthier a person is, the bigger the problems they are able to solve. I am always encouraging people to think bigger when it comes to money. If you want to just be able to provide for yourself, there's nothing wrong with that, simply get yourself a high-paying job. But if you want to tackle issues like crime in your community, global diseases and educating the next generation, you're going to need a lot more than a monthly pay cheque to be able to do so. Michael Omari, better known as the UK rapper 'Stormzy', is famous all over the world for his music. But he is also just as famous for his charity work, including the Stormzy Scholarship, which funds education for Black students at Cambridge University, and his pledge of £10 million over ten years to fight racial inequality in the UK. This is what I wish for you: that you are able to build your wealth to the point where you can change not just your own life, but the lives of those around you.

There is value in service

Something I think our generation has lost is the idea that there is value in service. Look at how much we celebrate the wealthiest and the most famous in society. If someone has made a million pounds, everyone wants to be friends with that person. But if a person says they've given days of their life in volunteering or raised thousands of pounds for charity, we do not glorify them nearly as much. What people need to realise is that charities are businesses just like any other for-profit company. The only difference is where their money comes from. Rather than relying solely on selling products and services to customers, they also have to rely on funding and donations to market and sell their services. Look at the revenues of the biggest charities in the world and you will see that they are not slouches. Save the Children made nearly £1 billion in revenue in 2021 alone according to GOV.UK, which is more than many companies did over the same time period. So there is value in helping others, not just for the people you are helping but also for yourself. The feeling I get from making money is good, and I of course need money to keep my business going and support my family; but it does not compare to the knowledge that I am making an impact by giving my time or energy to someone else. So I encourage everyone to get their money right and gain control of their finances. But the ultimate goal is to be able to change the life of someone else.

Giving to charity

You might not be at a stage where you can give to huge, global causes right now, but that doesn't mean that you have nothing to offer them. I think everyone should donate to charity if they can, but you don't necessarily have to give money. If you don't have any money, you can always give your time. You can volunteer at your local food bank or soup kitchen. You can apply to food poverty charities like the *Trussell* Trust, or do an internet search for local food banks in your area. If you don't have time to go out to volunteer you could always give some time to a charity like the Samaritans, which provides over-the-phone listening services for people experiencing difficulties in their lives. Giving your time is just as valuable as donating money, as these charities actually need people to volunteer in order to be able to provide their services. If you are time-poor and would rather help with what you have, buying a little extra at the supermarket and adding it to a food donation box – normally located near the tills in most medium to large supermarkets – is a great way to give back. You can also have a look in your cupboards at home and see if you have any packaged or tinned items that you don't plan on using. You don't have to wait until you have millions in the bank before you start giving to causes you care about. You can just pick one or two and get started today. It all counts.

What is the mark you want to leave on this world?

I have helped countless people extricate themselves from debt, get on the property ladder, invest and pass their assets on to their loved ones. I have reached people all over the world at events, via social media, on television and in the media. I was not born with any of the skills to do this; in fact I am still learning. And a big reason why I am doing it all is to show others and the next generation that it is possible to achieve your dreams while helping others to achieve theirs in the process. Think about the world as it exists today. What issues do you think about most? Maybe you have had a loved one in the family pass away from a preventable disease, or you have encountered discrimination in your place of work. Which problems do you feel, if solved, would improve the quality of life for people everywhere? This could be climate change, sustainability or global education. Decide on the thing you would like to dedicate your life to changing and go for it. Think big, but start small. One of the difficulties when it comes to truly solving problems in the world today is the fact that there are so many of them, and social media can make you think you need to be worrying about a different problem every week. If you can discipline yourself to focus on the small number of things where you can actually make a positive impact, you will be at a huge advantage compared to everyone else. I am greatly inspired by the life of Nelson Mandela, and how he managed to overcome being put in prison and suffering discrimination in apartheid South Africa to become the first Black president of the country. If we can all be as dedicated to specific causes as he was, I believe that we will be able to change the world.

Let me tell you a story about the mark I want to leave on the world

The mark I want to leave in the world is to let people know that you can achieve anything you put your mind to, and that you're not defined by your situation. That's the biggest thing for me. I tell people that I grew up in poverty. And today, rich people are paying me to tell them what to do with their money. I left school with four GCSEs. But today I'm an educator, and I educate people about money in the UK and across the world. I didn't do great in English or maths. I'm one of those people who uses Grammarly to make sure that their spelling is good. But here I am, being paid to write a book! The point I'm making is that if I can do it, you can do it. Don't get me wrong: there will be hurdles, there'll be barriers, and it will be difficult at times. But if you stay consistent, have a goal and work towards it, you can achieve it. I want this to be my legacy. This is what inspires me to continue to succeed.

I also want to leave a legacy for my family, my community and the people who engage with my content. It's about making sure that when I'm gone I'll leave behind a generation that will talk to their children and grandchildren about money, finance and investing. I also want to change the way people look at who can be an expert. It's very rare to see a person from my background and ethnicity in these spaces, compared to entertainment and sport. So I'm glad I'm able to make it cool to be an expert in finance, or science or any other educational sector.

I want you to understand that you can make it no matter what your background is. You can be your authentic self, and your authentic self is acceptable in these rooms. When

I first started in this field I tried to change the way I spoke and dressed, but today I speak in a way that's comfortable for me. So whatever you want to leave to the next generation, go ahead and do it! If I can do it, you definitely can.

Outro

I just wanted to say a big thank you to everyone who has bought *Get Your Money Right*. If you've come this far, thank you for buying it, getting through it and believing me. Thank you for trusting me to share these financial lessons with you and for supporting my dream of being a financial educator. I hope you have learnt from this book how money works, where it comes from and how to manage and invest it.

It's very important to me that I made this information available in affordable book form because good financial advice can be expensive, putting up a barrier for people who just want to learn. Within these pages I have shared all the lessons I have learnt in my career to date. But don't stop here; there is much more to learn about your finances. There are some principles which will always stay the same, but many of the rules and technologies will change over time. So use this book as a stepping stone for your future financial knowledge.

As I have said at various points, I come from humble beginnings, and I hope to be a role model to anyone who would like to turn their life around and inspire others. This is the mark that I would ultimately like to leave on the world. So if even one person reads this book and it inspires them to change their life for the better, then it will have done its job. Thank you so much for reading.

Acknowledgements

Writing has never been my strong point and throughout my journey I never felt I could write a book. I have thoroughly enjoyed this process and I wouldn't be the Emmanuel I am today without these people.

First and foremost I want to thank God, because without Him none of this would be possible.

My parents for their sacrifice and giving all they had to make me the person I am today. Thank you and I love you.

My wife, my best friend and business partner, thank you for always supporting me through my ups and downs, I didn't get to this point without you. I love you to infinity + 1.

My children for being the reason I keep pushing – I want to show you anything is possible and encourage you to continue to dream big. Daddy loves you.

Timi Merriman-Johnson, without your talent, knowledge, dedication and hard work this book wouldn't be possible; thank you for helping me from beginning to end to get it over the line. It was a pleasure working with you.

My sisters Sarah and Josephine, you mean the world to me.

Thank you for always believing in me and encouraging me to be the best version of myself. I love you both.

My family and friends, thank you so much for all your support and believing in me throughout the years. It's all love.

My Akwa Ibom Family, I love and appreciate you all dearly.

To my spiritual leaders thank you for all your advice, guidance and support throughout my life. Special mention to Uncle Muyiwa, Uncle Eddy, Pastor David, Pastor Sackey, Pastor Dapo, Pastor Edwin, Pastor Victor, Pastor KariKari, and Pastor Mbakwe and Mrs Mbakwe.

My Mandem all the way from Sunday school to now, My Greenwich Uni crew and ANC youngers, thank you all for your support, I hope I made you all proud.

My cousin Ese, this is our book.

Special shoutout to OJ, Wale, Teefy, Tayo, Henderson, Seye, Eman O, Sam A, Nelly, Victor, Nana, Novo, AJ, Jeremy, Joylene, Seun, Vicky, Caroline, Tinuke, Antoinette, Phil and Sarah, Michael Barry, Paul Mundy-Castle, Hakeem Sattar, Regina Tetteh, Shane Wheeler and Richard Stead. You helped me grow from a boy to a man and I appreciate every one of you.

My agent Sam, my biggest fan, thank you for taking a chance on me and trusting me. Your endless support and encouragement has been nothing short of amazing. Thank you for believing in me, seeing my vision and working tirelessly to make my dream a reality.

To Oscar, there are not enough words to say thank you for your belief in me and making this dream come true. From the first time we spoke till now you have been a constant source of encouragement. Thank you for all your hard work and support (I wouldn't be here without you).

To my finance industry and financial influencers family, thank you. I wouldn't have made it this far without your constant support – Mohammad Uz-Zaman, Jerran Whyte, Makala Green, Dineo Ledwaba-Chapman and Seun Balogun, to name just a few.

To those that have helped me on my entrepreneur journey: Bola Sol, Bianca Miller-Cole, Byron Cole, Daniel Moses, Raphael Sofoluke, Remi Ray, Bose Gbago, Kia Commodore, Fola Sogbesan, Anna Williamson, Delia Renee and Funmi Akinola. Thank you for helping me on this journey, I have gained so much from having you all in my life.

My Instagram family (The Eman Effect UK), my clients, and colleagues for your encouragement, likes, loves, shares and supporting me on my mission. I am forever grateful.

Finally, my sincere thanks to the entire team at Harper-Collins, especially my editor Bengono Bessala who saw the vision and went for it. It has been an absolute honour to work with you to bring this book to life.

It takes a village to raise a child and this is a small mention of my village: my success and all I have been able to achieve would not have been possible without all of you. I am forever thankful for your love and support while I have undertaken this process, the time, space and patience you have given while juggling my world. It has been a journey like no other and I am eternally grateful.